PRAISE FOR
THE EVANGELIZATION EQUATION

If you are looking for a watered-down definition of evangelization that refuses to speak the truth that within the Catholic Church is the fullness of Christ, then don't pick up this book. But if you want a real understanding of the mandate of the Gospels to convert our culture and bring souls to Christ, then this is the book for you.

—ROBERT P. LOCKWOOD,
former president of Our Sunday Visitor and
Director for Communications, Diocese of Pittsburgh

Fr. Wehner's research gives a broad explanation of the new evangelization that will prepare and challenge the reader to become a major player in evangelization.

—MOST REVEREND ROBERT J. BAKER, S.T.D.
Bishop of Birmingham, Alabama

Fr. Werner has written a very readable and yet comprehensive explanation of what the "new evangelization" is and, just as importantly, what it is not. *The Evangelization Equation* provides helpful clarification and practical considerations for all concerned with answering the Church's call for a new evangelization.

—MOST REVEREND PAUL J. BRADLEY
Bishop of Kalamazoo, Michigan

In this thought-provoking book, Fr. Wehner challenges the disciples of Jesus today to engage in the new evangelization to get people excited about their faith again—an enterprise which surely makes the challenge of Jesus as real as the day He set His commission alive.

—MOST REVEREND DAVID A. ZUBIK
Bishop of Pittsburgh, Pennsylvania

The Evangelization Equation will be a valued resource for priests, deacons, seminarians, pastoral workers, and members of the lay faithful. Fr. James Wehner has made a timely contribution through this very accessible introduction.

—Most Reverend Paul S. Coakley, S.T.L., D.D.
Bishop of Salina, Oklahoma

The Evangelization Equation presents a hard look at our current state of affairs—what's working and what's not—and proposes a way forward. Evangelization is not optional, and it's not primarily the clergy's job. This book should be required reading for any Catholic called to the apostolate, and that means all of us.

—Mike Aquilina
Vice president of the St. Paul Center for Biblical Theology

Fr. Wehner presents what is going on with the new evangelization in many parts of the United States. He has a compelling and comprehensive grasp of the topic, and presents the material in an enthusiastic and convincing manner. This treatise will prepare you to join in this new evangelizing mission for our Church today.

—Most Reverend Eduardo A. Nevares
Auxiliary Bishop of Phoenix, Arizona

As someone very interested in evangelization I recommend this book for those committed to the new evangelization that John Paul II and Benedict XVI have called us to. Fr. Wehner has an excellent set of principles to be used in effective evangelization beginning with the fact that we must love the people that we are trying to evangelize. It is a practical and helpful book for evangelizers!

—Most Reverend Michael J. Sheehan, S.T.L., J.C.D.
Archbishop of Santa Fe, New Mexico

The Evangelization Equation:

The Who, What, and How

THE
EVANGELIZATION
EQUATION:

THE WHO, WHAT, AND HOW

by Father James A. Wehner, S.T.D.
Rector and President
Pontifical College Josephinum

With a Foreword by Cardinal Donald Wuerl

EMMAUS
ROAD
PUBLISHING

Steubenville, Ohio
A Division of Catholics United for the Faith
emmausroad.org

Emmaus Road Publishing
827 North Fourth Street
Steubenville, Ohio 43952

Library of Congress Control Number: 2011921104
ISBN: 9781931018692

Cover design and layout by
Theresa Westling &
Nicole Thomason

DEDICATION

I was raised in a German ethnic neighborhood called Troy Hill on the North Side of Pittsburgh overlooking the Allegheny River, one of three rivers which contribute to the cultural heritage in the Diocese of Pittsburgh. My home parish, Most Holy Name of Jesus Church, is located in the center of the neighborhood. An adjacent chapel, called Saint Anthony Chapel, boasts of having more relics of saints than any other church outside of Italy. It was in this experience, where faith and culture were partnered, that I would discover my vocation to the priesthood.

Growing up as an altar boy, participating in Eucharistic processions in the neighborhood, learning about my German heritage, cultivating a real devotion to the saints, watching people truly live their Catholic faith is what evangelization is all about, at least to me. I received a "living faith" from parishioners who made all of Troy Hill a sanctuary where people praised the Lord.

I dedicate this book to the good people of Most Holy Name Church who first taught me to love my faith. In loving my faith, the Lord awakened in me a desire to be a parish priest so that I too could pass on a living faith to the next generation. I have always attempted to be the priest people deserve and expect.

Presently, I have the privilege of serving as Rector of the Pontifical College Josephinum, founded initially to be a seminary for German-speaking seminarians who would later become parish priests serving German immigrants throughout the United States. Today, the seminary formation program has embraced the "new evangelization" as the goal by which priestly formation is structured. In many ways, I consider present-day reflections about evangelization to be influenced by the seminarians who love their Church and want to be spiritual fathers for the flock. Their witness to me has been somewhat of an ongoing evangelization of my notion of priesthood, pastoral ministry, and conversion.

Our country is thirsting for the truth, a truth understood by our forefathers as coming from our Creator. Something has been lost. In a desire to protect the rights of everyone, the dignity of peoples has been cheapened, American culture has been poisoned, and people have forgotten where those rights originate. I dedicate this book to my mother who survived the brokenness of society and provided a home for my brother and me, resulting in our growing to be the men we are today.

There are so many problems one could list that must be solved, but none of them can be solved unless God is put at the center, if God does not become once again visible to the world, if he does not become the determining factor in our lives and also enters the world in a decisive way through us. In this, I believe that the future of the world in this dramatic situation is decided today: whether God—the God of Jesus Christ—exists and is recognized as such, or whether he disappears.

— Pope Benedict XVI

TABLE OF CONTENTS

✝

FOREWORD
THE EVANGELIZATION EQUATION:
The Who, What, and How

Shortly after Pope John Paul II approved the *Catechism of the Catho-lic Church*, the bishops of the United States created a committee of bishops who would oversee the implementation of the Catechism in our country. We understood this committee to be an aid to publishers in confirming the content of resources that would be used in the faith formation of our people.

The reason for this effort was the clear indication that nearly two generations of Catholics could no longer explain the basic tenets of the faith. When Catholics are unable to understand their faith, they often stop practicing the faith, search for it elsewhere, or simply go through the motions without ever really bringing faith in the practical aspects of everyday living.

Pope John Paul II, noting this worldwide phenomenon, began to address this pastoral situation with a call to a new evangelization. A significant dimension of this new evangelization is to discern how faith relates to culture, to determine the role of the Church in society, and for Catholics to rediscover their proper contribution to society. Pope John Paul II created the Pontifical Council for Culture to study these situations.

In *The Evangelization Equation: The Who, What and How*, Father James Wehner makes the case for the new evangelization and he does so with all the ease of the teacher who has mastered his subject and all of the conviction of the priest who loves his mission. Here we find a systematic, clear, engaging and inspiring explanation of the new evangelization. His reflections help us better to understand the cultural climate in which the Church in the United States lives and the challenges that it sets before us.

Recently I was on a plane in which a young man who was seated next to me began a conversation asking where I was going. I, in turn, asked him what was the purpose of his flight. He replied that he was going to a First Holy Communion of his niece. I said this should be a very happy occasion. He said, "Not for me. I am going because it's my younger brother's kid and because my mother called to tell me she expects me to be there." For the next two hours, we talked about the Church's understanding of the Eucharist, Holy Communion, and the Mass. It was clear to me that, while he claimed to be Catholic, he had no understanding of the faith. As we reached our destination, he said to me, "Father, thank you for taking the time to talk about Mass. This Holy Communion thing is cool." Then, somewhat embarrassed, he said, "I mean, great."

The new evangelization seeks to encounter people where they are and to bring them closer to Christ. The pastoral situations the Church encounters are moments of challenge and great opportunities for us to share our faith. Pope Benedict XVI has clearly asked the Church to consider once again the mission of the new evangelization. The Synod of Bishops will take up this topic in 2012 because of the urgency and opportunity present throughout the world but certainly here in the United States.

The reflections that Father Wehner provides in this resource seek to inspire conversation needed in all aspects of ecclesial life. We are the Body of Christ. All of us have a responsibility to undertake the mission of the Church according to our vocations and the generous gifts given to us by the Holy Spirit. It is my sincere hope that this engaging, well written, thorough, and theologically solid resource will create an even greater enthusiasm for the new evangelization and thus to manifest the Kingdom of God in our great nation.

Donald Cardinal Wuerl
Archbishop of Washington

ACKNOWLEDGMENTS

My reflections on the new evangelization really stem from the apostolic ministries of Pope John Paul II and Pope Benedict XVI. Pope John Paul II kept the promise made during his inaugural homily when he announced the Church's relevance in modern day society and how the Church needs to be involved in the affairs of man. His pontificate changed the way people saw the Church; it changed the very meaning of evangelization. Likewise, Pope Benedict XVI continually instructs bishops, ambassadors and diplomats, heads of state, and the clergy and lay faithful about the rightful and proper relationship between faith and culture.

I must acknowledge, in a most particular way, my former bishop, Cardinal Donald W. Wuerl, who asked me to pursue doctoral studies in Rome. His encouragement led me to discern the theological nature of evangelization and how the bishops of the United States were approaching the concept of evangelization in their writings as a conference of bishops. The Cardinal also assigned me as the Rector of Saint Paul Seminary in Pittsburgh, where I was called to integrate evangelization into the work of forming future priests for the Church. This effort continues to be an inspiration as I serve the seminary community at the Pontifical College Josephinum.

Emily Stimpson, a prolific writer who contributes to *Our Sunday Visitor*, assisted me by providing a good edit of this book. She also provided much of the information in Chapter Five, illustrating the practical implications of evangelization by method and example. She does great work for the Church in sharing her insights, talent, and knowledge. I appreciate her tremendous contribution to this book.

Finally, as I noted in the previous page, the seminarians of today have a real sense of evangelization by intuition and zeal. I often see older members of various presbyterates challenged by the younger priests and seminarians that create in them a certain anxiety. I must say that our seminarians today have a passion for understanding how the Sacred Liturgy is a source for evangelization; how popular piety and devotion to the saints ought to be cultivated among the faithful; how orthodox and pastoral preaching should not be avoided for fear of alienating people. The Church is already in good hands with the priests of today and will certainly be in great shape with our future priests. I would like to acknowledge the seminarians at the Pontifical College Josephinum as true renaissance men willing and eager to be priests of Jesus Christ!

Introduction

Math and Mystery

Let's begin with a test. We'll make it multiple-choice.

When you hear the word, "evangelization," what's the first image that comes to mind?

A. Two men dressed in black pants, white shirts, and narrow black ties traversing your block?
B. The earnest face of a friend, sipping coffee, and inquiring if you've accepted Jesus Christ as your Lord and Savior?
C. An energetic preacher, standing in front of a large crowd, passing out tracts on the "sinner's prayer."
D. Sunday Mass at your parish.

Let me guess . . . your first answer wasn't "D."

Despite forty years of papal documents since the Second Vatican Council, prolific pastoral statements from the bishops of the United States, writings from committed lay faithful, and despite the fact that the Church's primary mission for two thousand years has been to spread the Good News, the concept "evangelization" still isn't a "Catholic thing"—at least not in the minds of most Catholics. The Church at every level has urged Catholics to get serious about evangelization, yet most lay faithful still do not have a grasp of what that means.

More than a few equate it with Protestant proselytizing. Some shy away from it, thinking faith a private matter, not to be discussed in polite company. Others think it's the job of the hierarchical Church or the work of paid diocesan staffers, but not a task for each individual Catholic. And others still think of it in terms of parish programs—Bible studies, faith-sharing groups, evangelization teams—but not as what takes place every time the Word is proclaimed, bread and wine become Body and Blood, and ancient words are recalled with reverence and awe.

Evangelical Protestants and Mormons may not see a Catholic Mass as evangelization, but they don't share Catholics' reticence about evangelization, either. It's not surprising that so many Catholics associate evangelization with Protestantism, for at times it almost seems as if they have the corner on the evangelization market in the United States. Whether they are going door-to-door to converse with random strangers, standing on street corners calling out for people to be saved, or convincing their friends to come to church with them on Sundays, members of these communities have been almost unstoppable in their enthusiasm for introducing the culture to Christ.

Their commitment is admirable, their dedication inspiring. Their efforts have borne good fruit and changed many lives. And yet for all those efforts, there are inherent limits on the good that can come forth from their work. No matter how much they do, no matter how many friends they bring to Sunday services, no matter how many altar calls they make, no matter how many people they get to pray the sinner's prayer, it will never be enough. It will never be what men and women truly and ultimately need.

What we theologically profess, even at Sunday Mass when we recite the Nicene Creed, is that the Catholic Church possesses the fullness of Christ's Gospel. Our efforts to evangelize, therefore, cannot be shy about spreading this Good News. The Catholic Church alone is the authoritative means by which the Gospel can fully be communicated. This is what Jesus Christ intended—a body that possesses the complete truth, bringing redemption to every believer.

Through the power of the Holy Spirit, the Church gives to the world all that is necessary for salvation. Only the Church possesses the whole truth about man, God, and the God-Man who redeemed the world. For only in the Church has that truth been passed down infallibly from generation to generation through the teaching power of the Magisterium—the bishops of the world in union with the successors of St. Peter. The Church also possesses the sacraments—the actual means by which those saving events are re-presented to every man and woman in every culture in every era.

So, why aren't Catholics more eager and bold like our Protestant friends? Is it because we have no idea about our own Catholic identity? Is it because we fear the accusation of being superior? Some speculate that we Catholics, particularly here in the United States, are passive because we do not want to "impose" our faith on anyone else. Yet, the Gospel that we believe in is a Gospel that brings purification to our society.

Meanwhile, what our Christian friends have to offer in other denominations is not the complete Gospel. So when a culture is evangelized by anyone but the Church, no matter how earnest or pious those evangelizers are, it does not receive the whole Gospel. It does not receive the whole Christ. It receives something less—sometimes something only slightly less, sometimes something so deficient it barely resembles the true Gospel at all.

But man was not meant to hear an impoverished Gospel. He was not meant to know only a fraction of the Good News or love a blurred image of the Christ. And in today's world, a world broken and battered by sin, error, loss, and loneliness, nothing but the whole Gospel, the whole Christ, will do. More than anything else right now, men and women need the fullness of truth, the fullness of faith, and only the Church, empowered by the Holy Spirit, can give that to them. The Church exists for no other reason than that.

That is one of the most fundamental truths about evangelization: *"The Church exists in order to evangelize."*[1] Pope Paul VI emphasized this point in his post-synodal exhortation *Evangelii Nuntiandi*. This document has become foundational for understanding the theological and pastoral nature of evangelization and the Church's mission deriving from it. The Church's sacred vocation, the vocation entrusted to her by Christ, is to "make disciples of all nations" (Matthew 28:19). Her primary mission is to preach the Gospel through Word and Sacrament. That is the true nature of evangelization. The Church was not established

---

[1] Pope Paul VI, Apostolic Exhortation on Evangelization in the Modern World *Evangelii Nuntiandi* (December 8, 1975), no. 14.

to be a social services organization, nor to act as a legislative lobby, and certainly not to generate endless hours of committee meetings about the color of a parish's pew cushions. In the work of preaching the Gospel, all (or at least some) of those activities may become necessary, but they should never become the primary focus of the Church's time or energy. Unfortunately, they often do, resulting in parishes that seem to have no missionary identity in their community. The parish simply becomes just another congregation among many.

If we can truly accept the proposition—*the Church exists in order to evangelize*—the focus, vision, and energy of a parish community will be correctly developed around the strategies which bring about evangelization. Without this focus, committees spend endless hours attempting to formulate mission statements, arguing about which organization should be doing what task, and leading our lay faithful into thinking they are "involved" in the parish because they attend committee meetings.

A correctly focused vision about the nature of the Church and her mission to preach the Gospel will ensure that the Good News is reaching the faithful. The Church's mission to evangelize, of course, is not limited to the initial proclamation of the Good News. Evangelization doesn't end once souls are converted and initiated into the faith. Evangelization is as much about nourishing and forming faith as it is about awakening faith. And through both the awakening and the forming, evangelization seeks to transform cultures as well as souls. It seeks to create a world governed by authentic humanism, a world that sees and reverences the human person as the image and likeness of God.

"The Church exists in order to evangelize." It's a good sentence, a true sentence. And yet it's not quite a complete sentence. The sentence does not answer the crucial question, "Evangelize whom?" The answer is "man!" The Church exists in order to evangelize *man*. And that brings us to the second fundamental truth about evangelization: If the Church exists in order to evangelize, then man exists to be evangelized.

That latter truth was always implied in the former, but it was Pope John Paul II who drew it out, using the mystery of the human person as the starting point of evangelization.

Just as the Church's highest purpose is to make God known and loved, man's highest purpose, his greatest destiny, is to know and love God. In his first encyclical, *Redemptor Hominis*, John Paul II reminded us that in God the mystery of the human person unfolds. We can truly know ourselves and our purpose only in relationship with Him. Through knowing Him, loving Him, and being with Him, we find the answer to the perennial question, "Who am I?"[2]

Placing man at the starting point of evangelization highlights that it is not enough for the Church to simply proclaim the Gospel; she must proclaim it in such a way that people actually hear it. Successful evangelization requires a deep attentiveness to who man is, what he desires, and what unique challenges he faces in entering into communion with God. It requires an attentiveness to and engagement with culture. This attentiveness lies at the heart of John Paul II's call for a new evangelization.

In the new evangelization, John Paul II saw the Church preaching Christ to men and women of today at the dawn of the new millennium. One element of that preaching, he believed, should be recovery—calling people back to the practice and traditions of the faith. But the purpose of that recovery in his mind was not to replicate something old, but rather to build something new, to give rise to a new culture, a new humanism that counters attempts to pursue happiness and progress without even a nod to God.

Since the death of Pope John Paul II, Pope Benedict XVI has continued the call for that recovery. He too has repeatedly sounded the trumpet for a new evangelization, noting that, "Man cannot understand himself fully if he ignores God," and that, "Only if a living awareness of the faith illumines our hearts can we also build a just society."[3] Pope Benedict's exhortations to bishops who meet with him in Rome clearly reveal his concern that the Church be the chief protagonist in promoting an authentic humanism. The Synod of Bishops that was convened

---

[2] Pope John Paul II, Encyclical on the Redeemer of Man *Redemptor Hominis* (March 4, 1979), no. 9.

[3] Pope Benedict XVI, "To Participants in a Seminar on Catholic Education" (April 1, 2006), *L'Osservatore Romano*, 17 (April 26, 2006): 5; "Post-Mass Address to the Parish Community" (March 25, 2007), *L'Osservatore Romano*, 14 (April 4, 2007): 8.

in October 2008 demonstrated the Holy Father's priority of placing the Word of God at the heart of evangelization: "*Only the Word can change the depths of man's heart, and so it is important that with it both individual believers and community enter into an ever-growing intimacy. Nourishing herself with the Word of God is for the Church the first and fundamental responsibility*" (Address to the Synod, October 5, 2008).

In recent years, Catholics in America have taken some important steps in heeding the call of Popes Benedict XVI and John Paul II. Across the country, many dioceses and parishes are proclaiming the Gospel with renewed vigor, lay apostolates are continuing to form, and more and more Catholic colleges are working to strengthen their Catholic identity. Over 50 percent of all parishes have implemented a program specifically aimed at evangelization, and similar numbers of dioceses have created offices of evangelization to help the parishes in this task.[4]

And yet, for all that, weekly Mass attendance still hovers around 23 percent. Less than 30 percent of Catholics go to Confession at all in the calendar year. Nearly half of all Catholics vote for politicians who advocate abortion and same-sex marriage. Conversions to the faith have not dropped significantly, but they have not increased either. And the second largest religious identifier in the country is the "lapsed Catholic."[5]

The facts are hard to dispute. Whatever we are doing to teach and spread the faith—it's not working! Or, at least, what is working isn't being implemented often enough or in enough places. Something is missing. Something isn't happening. There is a crisis in evangelization.

I believe we can make the argument that the Church, at the parish or even diocesan levels, has, in the past, attempted to identify itself too closely with culture. To make the Gospel accessible, to express the faith in terms that are understandable, and to make the Church relevant have all blurred the real force of evangelization—to preach the Gospel in and out of season. Instead, well-meaning catechists, pastors trying to preach without offending people, and parents wanting to instill values yet without making religious beliefs "black or white" have left us

---

[4] From a USCCB commissioned study conducted in 1999 by Dean Hoge and Rev. John Hurley (http://www.usccb.org/evangelization/data.shtml).

[5] Based upon 2007 data collected by the Center for Applied Research in the Apostolate (pewresearch.org).

Catholics in the United States with an identity crisis. We have tried to identify the Church too closely with our American culture rather than evangelize that culture from the sins we struggle with today.

The Church, of course, doesn't bear all the blame for this crisis. Many of her problems originate in another crisis, a crisis in the mind, heart, and soul of American culture. The two are connected. The crisis in evangelization cannot be resolved without attention to the crisis in the culture, and the crisis of culture cannot be resolved without first resolving the crisis we have in evangelization.

Unfortunately, there is no easy 12-step program for doing that. There is no one "right" formula for successfully carrying out the new evangelization and no one program to implement that will reverse the Church and culture's course. I definitely will not try to suggest that there is one easy answer. But certain fundamentals do exist that those responsible for carrying out the Church's mission of evangelization—particularly pastors and parents, directors of religious education, and those involved in faith formation—must understand if their efforts are to bear fruit.

When it comes to evangelization, the "who" and "what" give us the "how." *Who* is being evangelized and *what* evangelization means tell us *how* to evangelize. Those three variables are what this book explores—by looking at the culture in which the Church exists and which she seeks to evangelize, then by outlining the unchanging fundamentals of evangelization, and by exploring how they take shape in the new evangelization, I believe a roadmap—although not a formula—for implementing the new evangelization in America can emerge.

Each parish and each community that attempts to follow this roadmap will undoubtedly find short cuts and alternative routes that work better for them. Evangelization is a mystery, not a program. But it is a mystery to be lived, not just contemplated; a mystery to be experienced, not just talked about. And it is a mystery that the Church in America must live out.

There are certain tests we cannot afford to fail.

PART I

The Who

CHAPTER 1
The Reign of Reason and the Advent of the Absurd:
From Modernity to the Post-Modern

On any given Sunday in almost any given Catholic parish in America, more of the people lining the church's pews will have watched *American Idol* during the week than will have watched EWTN. More of the parish's teens will have played Guitar Hero than attended altar server practice. And more of the parish's families will have spent their evenings on the soccer field rather than sitting around a dinner table or praying a family Rosary.

As much as priests like me would prefer it otherwise, the primary influence on Catholics in America is not the Church. It's American culture. Even among the most devout and the most faithful, the culture, not the Church, has formed the way we think, what we value, and how we spend the hours in our days. And more often than not, it is the culture that has shaped the way we see the Church rather than the Church shaping the way we see the culture—which is why more than 75 percent of Catholics are not at Mass on any given Sunday morning. The culture has told them they don't need to be there or that there is something more important that needs to be done.

Obviously, that's even truer of those outside the Catholic Church. With some notable exceptions, the primary influence on Americans of almost every stripe—Protestant, Jewish, and the unchurched—is American culture. It's the air we breathe. Some of the air is good, some not so good. Most of us take in the good along with the bad. Both affect us profoundly.

Trying to evangelize anyone, Catholic or non-Catholic, without understanding the culture that has formed them is about as futile as walking through a city without breathing the air. It can't be done. And it is useless to try the impossible. Accordingly, if a basic premise of the new evangelization is that man exists to be evangelized, then the starting point for any discussion about the new evangelization is the culture that forms man. As we're focusing on the new evangelization in the United States, the starting point for our discussion is American culture.

A Culture of Cultures

Unlike German or Russian culture, the foundations of American culture are not the traditions or history of any one ethnic group or nationality. American culture is a culture of cultures, influenced by the various people that have made their way to this country over the past several hundred years, with each new wave of immigrants making their mark on what we eat, what music we listen to, and what values we espouse.

Today, numerous ethnic and economic subcultures exist in this country—African and African-American, Asian, Indian, Latino, Muslim, the wealthy, the working class, the inner city poor . . . the list could go on and on. But as long as that list is, it doesn't mean that America has no meta-culture, no culture that transcends ethnic and social groupings. It does, and that culture is structured by the founding documents of our country—the *Declaration of Independence* and the *U.S. Constitution.*

Those documents have shaped a country, and they have shaped a people who believe in the protection of individual rights. They also believe that perhaps the most fundamental right of any man or woman is the pursuit of happiness. This happiness is found in our pursuit of the truth. "We hold these truths to be self-evident . . ." Our nation professes its belief that "truth" is self-evident, something that can be discovered in our human nature. The Church, as well as others, refers to this pursuit of truth in human nature as the *natural moral law.* While individual rights and the pursuit of happiness can be found in the natural moral law, when that pursuit is not purified, when that pursuit denies the rights of others, when that pursuit becomes selfish rather than in service to culture, it poisons culture. The Church, therefore, understands her role as an evangelizing community, to be an agent and protagonist seeking to purify culture.

Those two beliefs of individual rights and the pursuit of happiness are constants in American culture, unchanging in their essentials. But how Americans understand individual rights and happiness has changed and will change. We owe the way we understand them today to the influence of two philosophies that have incarnated themselves in our culture: modernism and post-modernism.

We could easily devote a whole library's worth of books to analyzing the effects of modernism and post-modernism on American culture, but I'll leave such a thorough discussion to other authors. Instead, I want to do a cursory tour of where the culture is, using modernism and post-modernism as our guides. They are the hinges on which the culture turns, and understanding them is probably the quickest and most accurate way to grasp the culture that forms the "who" in the evangelization equation.

Science, Industry, and the Cult of Progress

Modernism, as a philosophy, is a product of the eighteenth century and the Enlightenment, which saw man as ingenious because of what he could accomplish with the use of his reason. The Industrial Revolution of the late-eighteenth and early-nineteenth century seemed to confirm the triumph of the power of man's reason. Modernization championed science, industry, and technology. Understandably, man was thinking pretty highly of himself.

Accordingly, people celebrated and glorified human knowledge. They began to see it as the key ingredient for progress and social transformation. Its proper application to every sphere of life was considered the answer to all the world's ills. If only man reasoned hard enough, they thought, if only the right system of government or economics could be devised, sin and suffering, hunger and disease, war and strife would all just go away.

When the influences of modernization and modernism are seen together, we can see an overall attitude called *modernity*. Mankind believed it could achieve Utopia. Science, industry, and technology were considered the only means by which progress could occur. Anything that was not scientific, not strictly rational, was seen as the enemy of

5

progress and a threat to the rights of man. From medicine and music to warfare and worship, the modernizers thought all that was needed was to bring things "up to date." Their motto was very much "out with the old" (i.e., traditions, values, and beliefs not scientifically quantifiable or justifiable) and "in with the new" (i.e., all that reason and science could produce or make possible). Science, industry, technology, progress, and reason became the basis of culture.

Modernization in itself is not so bad—as a matter of fact, one can see its contribution in constructing a good and healthy society. And modernism certainly has its pluses as well. Topping that list is the way it places man at the center of all activity. It recognizes that in the order of creation, man comes first. This is in harmony with Judeo-Christian revelation that man was created in the image and likeness of God. There is something different about him, something special that sets him above the rest of creation as its ruler. Because it recognizes that truth about man, modernism tries to use reason to encourage research, programs, and policies that make people's lives better. Sometimes those efforts succeed, and we reap the benefits—think optometry, dentistry, and sanitary sewage systems. Again, modernism has its strengths.

However, there are also significant problems with modernity. While modernity celebrates reason, it denigrates faith. It denies that men can know anything apart from reason. It denies Revelation.

Not surprisingly, modernity does not look kindly upon the Church, which champions both faith *and* reason. Also not surprisingly, the utopian schemes born out of modernity—Marxism, Communism, Fascism, and Nazism—have all sought to eradicate or marginalize the Church. Modernity sees the Church, with her ancient traditions and mysteries, as the antithesis of scientific and technological advancement. Many modernists also blame her for the problems plaguing man, for shackling souls with superstition and obstructing the exercise of freedom. To the modernists and their successors, the Church is, as Marx famously called religion, "the opiate of the masses."

With no God to offer meaning or truth to humanity, modernity enshrines technology instead, preaching that technology can unlock the secrets of the universe and help man find meaning and happiness.

That explains why for the past two centuries, we have devoted ourselves to constantly producing (and consuming) newer and newer forms of technology and products of technology. In 2007 alone, Americans spent $40 billion to lose weight, $96 billion remodeling our kitchens, and $155 billion to outfit our home theatres and stereo systems.[1] And we did so because of the promise of modernity, the promise that every new kitchen appliance, every new iPod, and every new anti-cellulite cream would bring us beauty, respect, pleasure, comfort, leisure time, or whatever else we sought. Modernity promises solutions through science and salvation through things. It limits happiness to this world and quantifies it in dollars.

The Enslaved Despot

The irony about modernity is that human reason is glorified to the point that man believes creating systems (e.g., political or economic) will result in solutions that will eradicate all his problems. Often, the opposite occurs, and man finds himself enslaved to the very system that was to free him (e.g., fascism, communism, liberalism). On the one hand, modernity accords tremendous power to man, crediting his reason with the power to change the human condition. But at the same time, it produces a culture of individuals who hide behind the things and the structures they create. This applies to more than just technology. It is also true of government, industries, and other institutions.

In other words, modern man doesn't look to himself to solve his problems or the world's problems, nor does he blame himself for those problems. Instead, he places the responsibility for correcting cultural failures or problems on "the system," such as governments, corporations, and institutions. Rather than help his poor neighbor pay the heating bill during the winter, he expects a government program to help him out. Rather than oversee his children's education, he leaves it all to the schools. It's a convenient way to live, requiring little work on his part and giving him someone to blame when things don't go as they should.

---

[1] www.campaignforrealbeauty.com; http://www.metrics2.com/blog/2007/01/09/us_consumer_electronics_revenue_will_surpass_155_b.html;http://blogs.consumerreports.org/home/2007/09/kitchen-remodel.html.

How often do we see this tendency within the Church, within our parishes? With people so caught up in their own schedules, everyone presumes the pastor or a parish committee will take care of everything. Yet, these same people lament how ineffective the Church is and are in awe of Evangelicals who seem to help everyone. Even though the Church speaks about evangelization and how all the baptized are called to proclaim the Gospel, this mantra still seems remote to them, and they leave the mission of the Church to the professionals.

Modern man's dependence on "the system," of course, doesn't mean that "the system"—or anyone else for that matter—has the right to dictate what he is to feel or believe. In fact, according to modernity, it's just the opposite. With a hat tip to the common good, modernity declares that no external force or structure can unilaterally or absolutely tell man what values he should hold. It functionally declares that man's individual judgments about the true and the good are infallible. The individual is made the sole arbiter of truth and the judge of his own actions. His reason is made king. Freedom, to the modernist mind, is the freedom to do almost whatever one pleases almost whenever one pleases.

The end result of all this is injustice. The culture is awash with goods intended to make life better, but because each individual determines for himself what "better" means, as well as how to use those goods, the goods are misused and abused. People pursue wealth in ways that leave others jobless, homeless, or hungry. People pursue pleasure through pornography, drugs, and other forms of corruption. They celebrate "choice" at the cost of degrading or even destroying another's life—through abortion, divorce, contraception, fornication, and homosexual unions. They seek medical cures at the expense of the weak, the vulnerable, and the unborn. Unintentionally, injustice becomes as much a hallmark of modernity as reason or science.

But "happiness" and "freedom" are pursued, at whatever cost.

The Post-Modern Backlash

A century ago, modernism still sounded like a great idea to most people. But then it actually started shaping the culture. Science advanced, technology developed, "superstition" and "hang-ups" were cast aside . . .

and children started shooting each other with automatic weapons in high school libraries.

Shootings like that at Columbine High School in 1999 only confirmed what most people had suspected for some time. Modernity couldn't deliver. The more it took hold of the culture, the more people suffered—not just en masse in gulags, but as individuals, as souls. Marriages broke up, depression reached epidemic proportions, and again, children were killing each other. A new barbarism had come to America's cities, and modernism, with all its rationality and reason, couldn't do a thing to stop it.

Enter post-modernism, stage left.

Even though traces of post-modernism can be found as early as the 1920s, "it was after World War II that the first unmistakable evidences of post-modernism can be discerned."[2] Beginning in the 1980s, post-modern thought took a firm hold of most graduate school programs in the United States. By the early 1990s, newly minted Ph.D.s, schooled in post-modern ways, ensured that post-modernism dominated the undergraduate experience as well. By 2000, post-modernism was out of the academy and into just about everything else—movies, music, books, and even shopping malls. Today, what once was a loosely connected critique of modernity devised by an obscure band of nineteenth- and twentieth-century philosophers is now one of the most, if not *the* most, formative force in American culture.

So, what exactly is post-modernism?

Essentially, it is a philosophy that says modernity got it wrong. Reason alone can't tell us everything there is to know, and it certainly can't solve all our problems. It also holds that technology and consumerism result in just about as many problems as they solve, that the present is not always better and wiser than the past, and that there needs to be some common idea of the good to check the barbarism of modern culture.

Of course, you might not get that from reading early post-modern philosophers. Most of them, from Nietzsche and Hegel to Foucault

---

[2] Thomas Storck, "Postmodernism: Catastrophe Or Opportunity—Or Both?" *Homiletic & Pastoral Review* (January 2001): 9–19.

and Derrida, weren't given to clear expression. Their books and papers were filled with phrases like this one of Ludwig Wittgenstein:

> My propositions serve as elucidations in the following way: Anyone who understands me eventually recognizes them as nonsensical, when he has used them as steps to climb up beyond them. (He must, so to speak, throw away the ladder after he has climbed up it.) He must transcend these propositions, and then will he see the world aright. What we cannot speak about we must pass over in silence.[3]

Nonsensical indeed, but that was the point. What the post-modernists essentially denied was man's ability to know reality or know truth. Some went so far as to deny reality and truth altogether. As an alternative, they called on individuals to exercise their consciences for the common good: "Be attentive, be intelligent, be reasonable, be responsible" was the gist of their solution.

On the surface, that solution doesn't sound all bad. And it's not. Like modernity, post-modernism is not rotten through and through. It has its pluses. It even has points of agreement with Christianity. Reason alone can't tell us everything; progress doesn't automatically occur with the flipping of calendar pages; and technology does not bring salvation. Post-modernism's critique of modernity is, in many ways, dead on.

The problem with post-modernism isn't its assessment of modernity. It's the assumptions that underlie it and ultimately render it unable to bring about the very things it says it wants to bring about—namely a kinder, more peaceful world.

An Impotent Critique

In the process of questioning reason's ability to know everything, post-modernism ends up denying reason's ability to know anything. Post-modernism wants to recognize the necessity of values, ethics,

---

[3] Ludwig Wittgenstein, *Tractatus Logico-Philosophicus*, §6.54 in *From Modernism to Postmodernism: an Anthology*, second edition, ed. Lawrence E. Cahoone (Hoboken, NJ: Wiley-Blackwell, 2003), 143.

and morality; but, because it rejects absolute truth, it cannot suggest what those values, ethics, and morality might be. It also rejects the foundation of moral values, holding on to modernity's rejection of the Christian God and its view of the Church as a threat to liberty, freedom, and natural rights. In short, post-modernist thought can appreciate the values espoused by the Church, but it rejects the authority by which those values are presented.

Post-modernism's problems are relativism and nihilism. Post-modernism is great at pointing out problems, but terrible at solving them. It longs for the spiritual, but denies any spiritual power that makes an absolute claim on truth. It wants to do good, but can't define what good is. It tries to reject the modernist tendency of being enslaved by technology and consumerism, but fails to do anything more than throw stones at a tank.

In practical terms, this is why the New Age movement, with its vague spirituality and loose morality, is booming. This is also why people clamor to build "green" homes or buy T-shirts from that benefit AIDS victims in Africa, but can't bring themselves to remain faithful in a relationship. Post-modernism is all about easy spirituality, easy morality, and easy counter-cultural living. It's cool to "be spiritual," to help others, and to recycle. It's not cool to profess belief in the Magisterium, to curb our sexual desires, or to embrace real poverty.

To the post-modern mind, fidelity to an unchanging, timeless Gospel is monolithic. It may sound nice, but such fidelity strips away my individuality, my sense of how things ought to be, and how I want to express my own personal faith in God.

Creatures of Culture: Modern and Post-Modern Catholics

Modernism and post-modernism are more than just philosophies. Acceptance of these philosophies leads to real world conditions with real world consequences. And those consequences affect the baptized almost as much (and often just as much) as they affect the unbaptized.

Pastors are busy. Directors of religious education are busy, too. But parishioners are even busier. Almost 80 percent are too busy to make it to Mass every Sunday. Even more are too busy to participate in a Tuesday night Bible study or a Thursday morning prayer group. As for daily Mass or Stations of the Cross, well, in most parishes, you're lucky if even the retirees show up for those anymore.

From the pre-schoolers on up, most American Catholics run the same race as those outside the Church—the race to succeed. Modernity defines success in strictly material terms, terms that can be measured. Money can be measured. Promotions can be measured. High marks on tests or victories in sporting competitions can be measured. Sanctity . . . not so much.

Of course, that's not to say that all Catholics willfully skip Bible studies because of greed and a compulsion to climb the corporate ladder. Far from it. Much of it is simply a condition of living in a culture that sets the terms for the race. There are expectations from bosses and schools, commutes to make, and bills to pay. People work hard. They're tired, and they don't understand why making it to Mass should be a priority. To make things worse, many priests are not catechizing the faithful about the obligations of Christian living, fearing the congregation simply won't listen or might even stop attending Mass.

There is much about our Catholic faith that many people simply do not understand. Perhaps, most fundamentally, they don't understand that the Catholic Church is not a political party with left wings and right wings. Many have bought into the culture's rejection of absolute truth and concluded that they can decide to which wing they want to belong. Many do not think the Church teaches anything absolutely or that there's any problem in disagreeing with what the Church teaches. In fact, recent data on American Catholics' beliefs suggest that only 43 percent take the Church's teachings into account when deciding the difference between right and wrong.[4] This explains why Catholics contracept at the same rate as non-Catholics (about 90 percent), but still blithely receive the Eucharist on Sundays.[5]

---

[4] Center for Applied Research in the Apostolate (CARA), "Sacraments Today: Belief and Practice among U.S. Catholics," (Washington: Georgetown University, April 2008). Available at http://cara.george-town.edu/sacraments.html.

[5] Based on 2005 Harris Poll, see http://www.nytimes.com/2006/05/07/magazine/07contraception.html?_r=1&pagewanted=5&oref=slogin.

Possibility Junkies
Catholics have picked up some of their misinformation from inside the Church (we'll talk about this in a moment). But much of their misinformation, much of their thinking about right and wrong, truth and reality, comes from the media. Like most Americans, Catholics are media saturated. They watch an average of thirty hours of television a week and spend six hours a day in front of a computer screen, but read a book for only twenty minutes or less a day.[6]

With young people, it's doubly so. With iPods, cell phones, Facebook pages, Internet chat rooms, computer games, and their favorite television shows, teens and young adults come close to spending more of each day in virtual worlds than in the real world. And mentally, they are rarely in one place.

A recent article in the *Chronicle of Higher Education* recounts one college professor's discovery that his students simultaneously inhabited an average of seven "places" at once—an average achieved by alternately working on a paper, watching a movie out of the corner of their eye, instant messaging with three different people, and listening to their iPod, all while surfing the Internet!

That professor, Mark Edmunson, explained his students' behavior by coining the term "possibility junkies."

They are, Edmunson explained, eager "to study, travel, make friends, make more friends, read everything (superfast), take in all the movies, listen to every hot band, keep up with everyone they've ever known. . . . They live to multiply possibilities. They're enemies of closure. For as much as they want to do and actually manage to do, they always strive to keep their options open, never to shut possibilities down before they have to."[7]

That's modernity's gift of technological consumption married to post-modernism's hesitancy to declare anything true—an inability to commit, to settle, to attend to one thing. That's partly why Catholics

---

[6] http://www.csun.edu/science/health/docs/tv&health.html; http://communitymeltdown.typepad.com/fromfattofit/2008/07/is-screen-love-your-first-love-your-real-love.html; http://www.nea.gov/research/ToRead_ExecSum.pdf.

[7] Mark Edmunson, "Dwelling in Possibilities," *The Chronicle for Higher Education*, vol. 54, issue 27, (March 14, 2008): B7.

can't bring themselves to show up on Sunday for Mass, and very much what most of those who do show up bring with them. This is also one of the biggest impediments to Catholics hearing and embracing the Gospel. The Gospel has become just one alternative among many, and one that needs to be internalized on a level that the fast-moving, post-modern mind rarely reaches.

The picture, however, isn't all bad. Catholics have picked up the good habits of modernism and post-modernism as well as its detriments. They know how to put plans into action, as well as to use the modern drive for success to do good works for the Church and their community. That very desire to do good is a hallmark of post-modernism. Teens want to go on mission trips to serve the sick. Parishes want to adopt fishing villages in Haiti through Food for the Poor. Volunteerism is "in."

And like the rest of the culture, Catholics thirst for God. Whether they're going to Mass or not, 98 percent of Catholics still believe in Him.[8] They want to know Him better. And they know that their life without God is not complete. That applies to the youth of our parishes as much as the grown-ups. Every other year millions of teens flock to World Youth Days. Amazing how in one breath people say the Church is outdated and then admire how millions of teenagers travel all over the world to hear and pray with an old man, the pope. They're looking for answers, and they're open to finding those answers outside of classrooms and textbooks.

A challenge for evangelization is communicating the Gospel in a language that makes the Good News accessible. In the communication age where people do find time to spend hours in front of a computer, how does the Church appeal to a people clearly searching for the truth but wanting to hear it on their own terms?

When I served as rector of a diocesan seminary, I had to explain to the seminarians that the Church expects them to learn philosophy before learning theology in order to teach them how to think conceptually. The Church uses conceptual language to describe such theological realities as grace, resurrection, and mystery, even though language itself

---

[8] CARA, "Sacraments Today: Belief and Practice among U.S. Catholics," April 2008.

is not able to capture the full meaning of what those theological realities convey to us in faith.

This is why the Magisterium, in particular, is always fine-tuning its use of language to convey what we Catholics profess to be true. For example, the bishops of the United States spent years reviewing the English translation of the Mass to determine if present language was truly communicating what we are praying. Modernity and post-modernism have affected the way people listen, hear, and understand. A false sense of rationalism has stripped away the conceptual thinking of people. Therefore, we only believe what we see, only hear what is communicated in a sound bite, and only want to understand that which is physical. And so, I strongly emphasize with our seminarians that we must always be careful in what language and methods we use to preach the Gospel in order for the faithful to truly grasp the full meaning of our faith. Yet, at the same time, we do not want to "dumb-down" the great mysteries of our faith. One challenge is this: When the Church stands before our world to announce the Kingdom of God, the Gospel of Jesus Christ—what do they see?

Our young people, like their parents, are doubtful that they'll find the answers in an institutional Church setting. They question institutions. They question authority. They question the Church hierarchy. And to be honest, the hierarchy in our country has had its share of difficulties and problems in recent years.

Abdicated Authority

One of modernity's most harmful after-effects has been an irresponsible passivity, that habit of looking to structures—organizations, institutions, governments—to solve problems. Throughout the culture, people have surrendered their own rightful responsibilities to those structures.

One can say that we have a crisis of authority throughout our society. Children dismiss the authority of their parents and teachers; people do not take seriously the authority of political, judicial, and governmental institutions; even the disrespect seen at little league games towards the umpires is a symptom. This tendency to question every action of authority, although not a bad thing in some cases, has undermined the basic value of trust needed in any community. Therefore, those in leadership become wary to exercise their authority fearing they will offend someone.

Unfortunately, that same irresponsible passivity has wormed its way into the Church. At the parish level, many priests have ceded their own pastoral authority to pastoral councils, committees, and other structures devised by social scientists to ensure "more effective results." At times, these groups are helpful, even necessary, but at other times, they reduce the parish's pastoral ministry to a political dance marked by infighting, favoritism, and other very un-Catholic behaviors. They also can direct the parish in ways contrary to Church teaching, implementing changes in liturgy, architecture, and catechesis but often not possessing the necessary knowledge or formation to do so correctly. And the pastor lets it all happen.

Even more problematic, however, has been that same phenomena among some of the country's bishops. Since 2002, we have been treated to headline after headline advertising that some bishop or other ceded his authority to his staff, to psychologists, or to the diocese's lawyers. The sex abuse scandal that has rocked the Church in recent years could have been averted, or at least minimized, if those bishops had pursued their role as shepherd more seriously than their role as administrator. Instead, far too many relied on consultative structures that modernism promised would make the Church more efficient, more effective, and more in-tune with the culture. And the results? Dioceses bankrupt, charitable works undone, children and families forever scarred, and the loss of trust from the faithful. The Church has paid a heavy price for "efficiency," and we may be counting the cost for a long time to come.

Post-modernism's hesitation to make any claims to absolute truth has also found its way into the Church. Theologians, religious sisters, Catholic university faculty, and parish priests freely and frequently dissent from official Church teaching on any number of doctrinal issues. Many among the lay faithful have heard so many different things about contraception, homosexuality, divorce, the all-male priesthood, even Confession, that they genuinely have no clear idea of what the Church teaches.

To make matters even worse, many Catholics go to parishes every Sunday where the priest may full well agree with the Church, but hesitates to say anything that might give offense to his congregation. Even the bishops squabble amongst themselves about how to deal with pro-choice Catholic politicians. Are they in a state of grave sin or aren't they? Should they receive Communion or shouldn't they? It can be confusing for someone who knows perfectly well what the Church teaches, let alone for a Catholic who may or may not make it to Mass on any given Sunday. Catholics, like everyone else in the culture, are looking for answers. And if we're not giving them the right answers, they will find the wrong answers elsewhere.

The culture has affected the Church in countless other ways, big and small, that go well beyond the scope of this chapter. From the decline in priestly and religious vocations to catechetical and liturgical experimentation to dabbling in problematic Eastern spirituality, modernity and post-modernism have more than left their mark on the Body of Christ. Bishops, priests, catechists, and teachers are fighting an uphill battle, and that fight has been hampered by institutional challenges from within. Lay staff are generally overworked and underpaid. Ordained and religious shoulder alone a burden it once took a rectory of priests or a convent of sisters to shoulder. And confusion reigns in far too many quarters. To put it bluntly, if things do not change, the crisis affecting other denominations will divide Catholics from the Church herself. Schism among the other denominations reflects a lack of authority or a misuse of it. The one, holy, catholic, and apostolic Church subsists in our Catholic Church. Hence, through our obedience to Christ, nothing will separate us from the love of Christ. However, we have a responsibility to purify the institutional Church of all that is not of God.

But—and this is a big "but"—that's exactly why the work of the new evangelization is so important. That's why it's not enough to just understand evangelization in some vague sense or keep doing the same old things we've been doing for so many years now. Modernity and post-modernism have created a host of problems for the culture and the Church, but they've also created an environment that is ripe for the Gospel. The culture is broken, and post-modernism, despite its recognition of that brokenness, can't offer any real solutions. And that is because the only real solution is Christ.

This, as I said before, is where we, as members of the Catholic Church, come in.

PART II

The What

CHAPTER 2

Foundations and Cornerstones:
The Essentials of Evangelization

Before America fell into the grip of post-modernism, Pope Paul VI called a meeting of the world's bishops. The year was 1974. Nine years had passed since the close of the Second Vatican Council, and change was in the air.

On one level, that change was marked by a renewed and almost unstoppable fervor to preach the Gospel. At the same time, however, there was a growing desire in America and elsewhere to use the Church and the Gospel as instruments of social change, to use one or both to further various political, economic, and social agendas.

Both desires came with their own set of problems. While enthusiasm about preaching the Gospel can be a wonderful thing, it can also do more harm than good if the methods of how it's preached undermine its message. That's doubly true when the Gospel is preached in a narrow or utilitarian way.

The Pope recognized the problems inherent in such an approach. He also knew that certain universal concepts exist in the work of evangelization—concepts that are always present, that originate with Christ and God's plan for salvation, and that do not contradict the Church Christ founded for the very purpose of preaching the Gospel.

Pope Paul VI called the 1974 Synod of Bishops to define those concepts.

The preparatory document for the Synod, the *lineamenta*, described a "crisis in evangelization"—a crisis that the methods of psychologists, social scientists, and other worldly "experts" could not solve. Instead, the *lineamenta* stated that the crisis could only be solved by the Church clarifying the basics of evangelization: What are they? What action steps must be taken? And what theological concepts must always be present?

The Synod didn't answer that first question. It produced no definition of evangelization. That came later, with Paul VI's apostolic exhortation, *Evangelii Nuntiandi*. There, the Pope gave three slightly different but complementary definitions. According to the document, evangelization is:

1. "the proclamation of Christ our Lord to those who do not know him, in preaching, catechetics, baptism, and the administration of the other sacraments."
2. "the carrying forth of the Good News to every sector of the human race so that by its strength it may enter into the hearts of men and renew the human race."
3. "bearing witness simply and clearly to God as he is revealed by Our Lord Jesus Christ, proclaiming that he has loved the world in his Son, and that in the Incarnate Word he has given existence to all creatures and has called men to eternal life."[1]

The Synod may not have produced those definitions of evangelization, but what it did do was clarify the theological principles underlying the work of evangelization. It gave the Church a theology of evangelization. Without grasping the theological nature of evangelization, the pastoral initiatives of parishes and dioceses can be reduced to programs or efforts that do not tell the whole story of Christ. Or, even worse, a Gospel that is doctrinally deficient.

Theology studies the Word of God as it has been revealed to us by God Himself. We believe that God's Word is timeless, unchanging, and completely true. Therefore, if evangelization is about preaching the Gospel of Christ, a Gospel meant for all times and in all seasons, then evangelization itself has a theological character. It is not simply a pedagogy of activities that promote *how* to teach the Gospel; rather it is the manner in which the Gospel is handed on from one generation to the next. If evangelization is to be authentic and complete, it must consider its theological foundation. This sort of talk can make some who are involved in ministry today nervous, because they see

---

[1] Pope Paul VI, *Evangelii Nuntiandi*, no. 17 (hereafter cited in text as EN.)

"theology" as simply an academic, classroom pursuit. However, a proper understanding of "theology" recognizes that everything we do as a Church is ultimately an expression of theology—the reception, study, and practice of our faith in God's revealed Word.

My argument is that evangelization must possess four theological foundations: a soteriological foundation, a christological foundation, an ecclesiological foundation, and an anthropological foundation. These tracts express in theological terms certain truths that come from the Gospel of Christ. What is contained within each of those foundations sets the parameters for all evangelization, including the new evangelization. They tell us why we're evangelizing, underscore the doctrines we must present, and give us the reasons for presenting those doctrines in the first place. They give us the basis for the "what" in the evangelization equation.

Once we grasp the theological nature of evangelization we can then embrace what Pope John Paul II would later call the "new evangelization." John Paul II, when he was still the Cardinal of Krakow, attended the 1974 Synod of Bishops. His proposal years later for a "new evangelization" grew out of the conclusions about evangelization reached at the Synod, and cannot be understood apart from them. The new evangelization, like all evangelization, must be rooted in the truths found within each of the four foundations in order for it to be both true and eternally effective.

When parishes attempt to strategize how they will be an evangelizing community or when individual Catholics try to discern how best to evangelize within their particular vocations, it is essential that there be a basic theological premise of what can never be compromised in our efforts to preach and live the Gospel.

So, what are the foundations of evangelization, the truths that all evangelization must proclaim?

The Soteriological Foundation of Evangelization

Soteriology is not the easiest word to understand in the Church's lexicon. Unless you're a theologian or an expert in Greek, the word *soterion* (to save) tends to conceal more than it reveals. However, the concept does remind us that "evangelization" must be understood from its theological character. In short, evangelization considers how God's revelation of Himself is a saving experience for mankind. Every act of divine Revelation is ultimately one of salvation. The 1974 Synod of Bishops emphasized the soteriological foundation of evangelization confirming that God has revealed Himself to men so that they might be saved. We hear and receive that message through the Church's work of evangelization.

Even more plainly: Through evangelization, we learn that God wants to save us. This may seem obvious, but what the Synod clarified is that we must never lose sight of why God made Himself known to us in the first place. It is all about saving us—from sin and evil. And the "way" in which mankind would be saved is just as important for understanding how we are to relate with God, how we love Him, and the manner in which we are called brothers and sisters in the Lord.

The message is simple, but essential. Countless philosophies and social systems, from nihilism and Communism to Freudianism and Marxism, deny God's existence and the possibility of eternal happiness with Him. They promise a kind of salvation, but it's a salvation limited only to this world and a happiness defined, for the most part, by material goods, by things. Evangelization counters that promise by declaring not only the possibility of eternal salvation and eternal happiness, but also that God wills it for each and every one of us.

Even more importantly, evangelization proclaims that God's plan of salvation for man is not generic. It's personal. God knows us, and wants to be known by us—which is why His Word became man. In the person of Christ, God makes Himself known to us.

We can, of course, choose to ignore God's offer. We can allow our reason to be warped by sin. We can ignore Revelation. We can deny the grace offered to us. But we also can accept that grace. We can accept Revelation, use our reason, and discover in Christ that God exists, that He is a Trinity of Persons giving Themselves to one another fully and without reservation in love, and that He wants to share His divine life with us. Evangelization allows us to discover that God is love.

The Why of History

God's desire for us to make that discovery is the starting point for evangelization. It's also the starting point for understanding the life and history of man. That's because we cannot consider any aspect of human life—not its trials and tribulations, and not its joys and triumphs—apart from God's will that all men be saved.

Life sometimes makes that hard to see. It's not always readily apparent what doing the dishes or painting the garage has to do with our salvation. It can be just as hard to see that salvation is the goal of our existence. The world can blind us to the real end God has for us, and lead us to start chasing after false ends, ranging from mere survival to the age-old temptations of money, sex, and power. The world can also offer false hope, promising freedom or liberation from injustice through means that either reduce God to a mere ideology or leave Him out altogether. But the soteriological foundation of evangelization dispels these temptations through the proclamation of a personal, relational God—a God we see in the face of Jesus, who calls us into communion with Him as a body of believers in the Church, and who sees every detail of our existence as important.

This call to salvation comes through a person—Jesus. But Jesus is more than the person who makes the call: He *is* the call. Jesus is the content of the message of salvation. His words and deeds are as much the Good News as is the message that God wills all men be saved—which is why Christ and His Church can never be seen as secondary aspects of evangelization.[2] They are both the content of evangelization and the primary means through which evangelization is accomplished and received. In other words, Christ and His Church communicate the truth about Christ and His Church.

The Holy Spirit and the Life of Grace

How man is able to accept divine Revelation, how he is able to believe in this revelation, how he is able to be drawn into the life of God,

---

[2] See J. Krol, "Reaching Youth and Inactive Catholics" (Intervention, 3rd General Session, September 30, 1974), *Origins* 4 (October 1974): 250.

is only possible by the grace of God. There is no human initiative, no tower that can be built, no scientific discovery or technological invention that can get us to heaven. The soteriological foundation of evangelization acknowledges that the Holy Spirit is the primary agent of evangelization. Ultimately, man can only come to know about the message of salvation because of the Holy Spirit. The Holy Spirit stirs the desire for truth and eternal happiness within each of us and leads us to question the meaning of our existence. The Holy Spirit also offers us the grace to accept that truth and assent to it with our lives. Knowledge of Christ's work and the mysteries of the faith is one thing; actually becoming a partaker in those mysteries is quite another. Without the Holy Spirit the latter is simply impossible.

What begins with the anthropological understanding that all men desire truth, happiness, and the good life intersects with the grace of God in the Holy Spirit that allows man to actually *believe* in what God reveals in Scripture, in the Tradition of the Church, in what the Magisterium teaches, and what the sacred liturgy celebrates, and to actually believe in Jesus Christ. Without this grace of the Holy Spirit, we are only left with data, a history of events to be studied, a community of people who profess belief in a set of ethical standards. Human arrogance, the reinterpretation of the Gospel, the refusal to adhere to the teachings of the Church, and the failure to observe the totality of our Catholic faith are consequences of not allowing the Holy Spirit to guide us.

This leads us to the final point of this section. Sin is a reality in all our lives. It cuts us off from the Lord and from one another. It prevents us from being happy, from loving, from living the lives the Lord wants us to live. God's plan for salvation, however, offers us *redemption* from our sins. Evangelization understands that salvation comes to us through redemption. God transforms physical evil and personal sin into something new. Through the gifts of the Holy Spirit, we receive a grace that binds up wounds and makes it possible for us to receive the gifts God wants to give us here and now.

While God is not the cause of evil and sin, in His own divine providence the permission for it to exist is truly a mystery. Yet, when lives are transformed from sin and converted to God's mercy, the amazing witness to God's love makes all things clear. This is what evangelization must proclaim. True liberation moves the person from being a slave to sin to being a new creation. This is why evangelization can never tolerate any existence of sin. When priests or anyone in ministry condone contraception, homosexual unions, and abortion, then the Holy Spirit is no longer the agent of evangelization. Man once again replaces the grace of God with arrogance. Liberation is only achieved when people embrace the totality of the Gospel. Our job is to help people carry the crosses that come with being disciples of the Lord. When people are faithful, then Resurrection will surely result, bringing with it liberation, freedom, and new life.[3]

At Sunday Mass we recite the Nicene Creed, professing that "for us men and for our salvation he came down from heaven." We all need to be saved. We are all sinners. We all struggle through life, individually and as a community. Evangelization recognizes this need for salvation. If either the evangelizer or the one to be evangelized docs not recognize the need for conversion, evangelization will be fruitless and incomplete.

The Christological Foundation of Evangelization

The soteriological foundation asserts that God wants all men to be saved by Christ and through the Church. The second foundation, on which evangelization rests, clearly and boldly asserts the *single* way in which salvation is achieved. It focuses on Christ Himself and His central role in how salvation is accomplished.

The Good News of evangelization is that God has made known to us in the person of Jesus Christ the mysteries of life and the purpose of life. God prepared the world for this Good News with a plan of divine Revelation that begins with the creation of the world itself. The Old Testament reveals God's ultimate plan in creating the world. Choosing and forming the people of Israel, who would be the first to receive the Word of God, ultimately prepared the world to receive this Word as a person, as man.

---

[3] Pope Paul VI, Homily, 3rd General Assembly of the Synod of Bishops (September 27, 1974), available in Latin at http://www.vatican.va/holy_father/paul_vi/homilies/1974/documents/hf_p-vi_hom_19740927_lt.html.

The christological foundation of evangelization tells us that there can be no salvation apart from Christ. There can also be no preaching of salvation apart from Christ. Salvation comes to us through the mysteries of His life—His birth, His preaching, His death, and Resurrection. Those mysteries reveal God's gift of salvation to us. They also accomplish salvation *for* us, and commission us to preach salvation to all men. When these mysteries don't reside at the heart of evangelical efforts, the salvation being preached can easily begin to resemble a salvation that depends on human efforts, not God's. Neither man nor any of his philosophies or politics can ever be the basis for salvation.

As a matter of fact, believers within the Church may even acknowledge their need to be saved but sometimes fail to understand that only in and through Christ can this be accomplished. The New Age movement has convinced people that there are many ways to be saved, converted, and freed from sin. This "pluralism" has even affected how some in the Church go out preaching the Gospel, which has only caused more confusion among our people. For evangelization to be truly effective, people must understand and accept that only through Christ has salvation been accomplished.

Preaching the Mysteries

The Gospel *of* Christ is truly the Gospel *about* Christ—who He is and how He comes to us. We use the word "mystery" in relating the Gospel to people. However, "mystery" does not mean we cannot understand. The word comes from the Greek and means that we are able to grasp the divine through physical encounter. The Word of God physically becomes man.

In considering this christological foundation of evangelization, we understand why God's Word becomes man. When we preach the Incarnation, we preach that two thousand years ago, in the town of Nazareth, an angel told a virgin that she would conceive the Son of God. We preach that nine months later, in a stable in Bethlehem, this virgin gave birth to Jesus Christ, the Word made flesh. And we preach that Jesus Christ, the second Person of the Trinity, is fully a divine person, possessing both a divine and human nature from the very moment of

His conception in that virgin's womb, hence truly like us in all things but sin. Evangelization teaches us that God's Word is indeed accessible—as it was for Mary. God breaks His Word into human experience. So, we must first understand that part of the Gospel in order to understand how that Word is experienced today, in the 21st century. The Bethlehem event is not simply a historical event of the past—it becomes the basis for how we receive Jesus Christ today.

Evangelization must bring to people today every aspect of who Jesus Christ is because God wanted the world to experience Himself through Jesus. So, evangelization will answer questions such as: Who is Christ? How did He deal with temptation? What are His teachings? Why did He have to suffer? What is the real meaning of the Resurrection? How does His life affect my life today?

Evangelization will then be able to bring every person into a direct relationship with Christ. And because we are human beings, the "relational" aspect of how we get to know other people must be considered in how we come to know Jesus Christ. The search for God begins with coming to know Jesus Christ—not academically, but personally. Coming to know any person certainly requires a sense of "knowledge" as well as "experience." In the Church there can be some tensions—how can we know Christ *and* experience Christ? Some emphasize one pedagogy over the other. Evangelization must consider *both* according to where that believer is in his faith formation.

The second mystery, to which the christological foundation of evangelization calls us, is the preaching of the ministry of Christ— the three years He spent actively teaching and healing on earth. Like the Incarnation, Christ's life and ministry reveal the Gospel. God fully communicated His will to Christ and to no one else. Christ's words and actions, therefore, convey the truth of how God calls us to live, to think, and to worship. They also convey the truth about how God calls us to evangelize. We preach the Gospel because Christ commissioned us to preach the Gospel, and we look to Christ's life as the model for all evangelization (EN 8). We also look to His words for the content of evangelization. And what those words do, over and over again, is proclaim the Kingdom of God.

The Kingdom of God was the central focus of Christ's preaching. The New Testament records His mentioning it 90 times. The phrase itself occurs 122 times. To preach Christ's ministry is to preach the Kingdom. It is to preach about who shall enter the Kingdom—the meek, the humble, the poor, those who suffer, and those who mourn. It is to preach what the Kingdom is like—a pearl of great price, a mustard seed, a field of wheat and tares. And it is to preach the law of the Kingdom— to love the Lord our God and to love our neighbor as ourselves.

The christological foundation of evangelization recognizes that the mystery of Christ's life can neither be understood nor preached apart from the mystery of the Kingdom, a Kingdom He covenanted to His disciples at the Last Supper, a Kingdom He inaugurated through His death and Resurrection, and a Kingdom that continues today through the communion of believers in the Church (EN 10). What evangelization introduces to us is the destiny God wills for all creation, for all men. The biblical and theological language of "Kingdom" is more about how God calls us to be in communion with Himself than a place. It is the experience of God Himself—a communion of persons, a communion of love.

The final mystery of Christ's life that evangelization must proclaim, the mystery upon which God's promise of salvation rests, is the paschal mystery. Christ suffered, and Christ died. He was mocked, beaten, and hung on a cross. After three hours on Calvary, breath left His body. After three days in a tomb, He breathed again. In the mystery of those historical moments, the Trinity is fully and finally revealed. God shows us the totality of His love, and the fullness of His self-gift. He exempts Himself from nothing. Just as all men suffer as a result of original sin, so too does Christ suffer as a result of sin—our sin. And just as death is the price all men pay for sin, so too is death the price Christ pays for sin . . . again, *our* sin. He gives everything so that we might possess everything—eternal life and happiness with Him (EN 9).

And that is the second reason why the work of evangelization requires that we preach the paschal mystery. Not only does it reveal more about who God is, but it reveals the meaning of our existence.

God raised Jesus Christ from the dead, and in doing so, He made a promise. To all those who accept Christ and to all who, like Christ, accept suffering and death with faith and love, God will grant the gift of eternal life. That, Christ reveals, is man's ultimate vocation. The paschal mystery reveals the goal of this life. It reveals our destiny.

Savior and Lord

True and effective evangelization requires preaching the mysteries of Christ's life. It also requires preaching the mystery of what He does for us, of who He is in relation to us. The scriptures testify to the many titles believers have given to Jesus—the Christ, Messiah, the Anointed One, Redeemer, etc. Each reveals something about who Christ is and how His mission is accomplished. In my reflection, there are two Christological titles that evangelization can easily embrace: Savior and Lord. As we profess in the Creed, "for us men and for our salvation he came down from heaven." To save us is, in fact, what He did and this indeed makes Him our Savior. What He saves us from and how He saves us truly makes Him the Lord. To destroy the greatest weapon of the devil—death—and to resurrect human flesh from this death into a beautiful, glorified body, which the apostles failed to even recognize at first, is indeed Good News for the human race. *You too will rise* is the message of evangelization. The fact that Jesus did not come back from the dead rather *resurrected* from the dead reveals the glory of God and the love He has for us. Christ indeed is Lord!

If society fails to admit the reality of sin or its consequences, then how will people see the need for a savior? If pluralism has taken hold of our society stating that many roads lead to salvation or that other saviors besides Jesus Christ can lead us to the truth, then how can we Christians preach the need for total conversion to Christ?" The ridiculous speculation about Jesus being a man who sinned like us, who had an affair with one of His own creatures, denies the revelation of God. To speculate that God has given other saviors besides Christ or that He will later give us another savior in the future beyond Jesus indicates that the Church needs to truly evangelize about the identity of Jesus Christ and what His mission has totally achieved. Evangelization must preach Christ as the *only* Savior and Lord who God has ever or will ever give to us (EN 27).

In today's culture, it's easy for believers to get caught up in the culture's habit of looking to human ingenuity and reason for solutions to our problems—that's the curse of modernity—thinking that if we only work hard enough and think hard enough, we can fix whatever ails us, from global problems such as war and disease to personal problems such as a daughter's refusal to eat.

But the mindset that man is the only answer to our problems dismisses the mystery of grace, scoffs at the idea of embracing the Cross, and underestimates the darkness of sin. It also sees the notion of Christ the Savior as either an emotional crutch for the weak or a poetic expression of our need for help.

It is clear for anyone actively involved in ministry today that people are in search of a true and authentic savior. The problem is where this search begins and where it often ends. Even for Catholics who practice their faith, modernity often causes a separation of faith from the social, temporal, and political spheres of culture. Therefore, they believe that the only true solutions to our moral problems will come from science, the government, or social agencies. The Church, they feel, can make us feel good through a Gospel of the future, in the after-life where Jesus is awaiting us. Because of this mindset, held by so many, effective evangelization must lead people to experience Christ as our Lord and Savior in the present moment.

Overcoming that mindset is a huge challenge for the Church today, which is why the work of evangelization must include preaching that salvation comes from Christ alone. His life and work accomplished salvation for us, and His grace extends it to us. Human ingenuity will never solve the real problems that plague men. It can never fix the sickness at the heart of our race—that healing comes only through Christ to those who ask for His grace and accept their crosses.

That's also why the goal of evangelization cannot be to create some social or political system that claims to free man from all suffering. Not only does that make the Gospel a utilitarian instrument, but it also denies the truth that suffering can actually be an instrument of salvation. Christ didn't avoid suffering and death. He conquered the effects of them in rising from the dead. Likewise, by following His example, each of us hopes to receive the same gift: liberation from death in eternal life.

As Savior, Christ destroys the greatest weapon of the devil—death. Christ embraced the suffering which resulted from human failure and transformed that suffering into new life. Christ indeed is the New Adam. We see in Him how human life is destined for glory. The disciples saw the gloried Christ and heard the invitation—you too will rise! Embracing the Cross rather than walking away from it is what evangelization announces.

The Resurrection of Jesus from the dead reveals that He is Lord. There is no sin, no evil, no force on earth, and no force in the netherworld that can prevent the manifestation of the majesty of God, subvert the coming of His Kingdom, or even destroy His Body. The Resurrection promises us the same—we too can be "lords" over sin, death, and evil. The lordship over human life is only found in Christ. There is no human institution that can replace the lordship of Christ, but evangelization can bridge the human effort with the divine initiative. Faith does not have to be separated out from society—it can and should be the force that brings truth to people and shows them what they can accomplish in Christ. Christ is Lord of all creation, and we share in this lordship only by the grace of God which evangelization introduces to the believer.

The Ecclesiological Foundation of Evangelization

The soteriological foundation confirms why God has created us and the destiny of salvation that awaits us. The christological foundation of evangelization requires that Christ be preached—the One who indeed saves us. The ecclesiological foundation of evangelization establishes how we encounter Jesus Christ and how God's plan of salvation is experienced—through and in the Body of Christ. The ecclesial foundation of evangelization begins with this fundamental truth: God is not alone. Ever! He is Three Persons, all sharing the same nature, and existing together in eternity in a perfect communion of love. He is a family, a community which is one of the reasons why salvation comes to us through a community, the Church.

At the 1974 synod, the bishops insisted that evangelization must counter the false idea that the Church is an option—something that may or may not play a role in our salvation if we want it to. Membership in the Church, they reiterated, is not a personal preference. It's part of God's plan. And it's essential to both the act and message of evangelization.

The Church in Salvation History

Long before Christ passed the keys of the Kingdom to Peter, the place of the Church in God's plan was foreshadowed in the Old Covenant by the Israelites, the Chosen People of God. There, although God revealed Himself to individuals through individual experiences, He always made it clear that He gave His Revelation for the community as a whole. The triple institutions of priests, prophets, and kings; the gathering of the Chosen People into twelve tribes; the revelation of Law and Covenant; the sacrifices of the people; the intervention of God in the events of history—all of these point to a preparation for a new, eschatological community that would fulfill what was begun by God in the Old Testament.

Later, in the New Testament, God revealed that the mysteries of salvation will be communicated through the Church. He also revealed that each of us will enter into these mysteries through the Church. In the Church we are born again in Baptism. In the Church, Christ communicates His life to us through the Eucharist. In the Church, we receive forgiveness for our sins and the grace to overcome temptation.

This revelation unfolds through Christ's preaching and through His inauguration of the Kingdom of God. It takes form—the Church takes form—as the apostles preach the Good News. The Church instituted by Christ and built on the apostles is the visible, historical, and concrete community that manifests the Kingdom. The Church is, in fact, a sign of God's Kingdom here on earth. The Second Vatican Council acknowledged her as the "primordial sacrament" of salvation. That means she is the sign of God's plan in the world, a mystery that can never be reduced to a mere institution. That explains why the unity of the Church, both internally in matters of faith and doctrine, and externally as a community, is so important for understanding how evangelization drives the mission of the Church. The unity, or "communion," among believers reflects the unity of the Trinity and the communion of the Father, the Son, and the Holy Spirit—unity that all mankind is called to embrace.

On This Rock

As the Body of Christ, in whom Christ's own Spirit dwells, the Church reveals Christ in the world. Whoever finds her, finds Him. Moreover, as the bridge between man and God, she doesn't just communicate or make possible the mysteries of salvation. She is one of those mysteries. She is part of the Gospel. This is the awesome theological reality of divine Revelation—man not only is the object of Revelation, he becomes a part of it. Abraham, Moses, the prophets, and kings all are agents of God's Revelation to us.

That same truth applies to the apostles and their successors. They are not only recipients of Christ's command to preach and baptize all nations, but they are also what divine Revelation intends. The apostles, their successors, and the institutions they form are what Jesus Christ intended to allow the fullness of His Gospel to be transmitted to all generations. The apostolic college assures us that what we believers hear and receive today is the same Gospel of yesterday—unchanged, complete, and not manipulated. Indeed, while Christ calls all believers to preach and bear witness to the Good News, the task belongs first and foremost to the bishops, the successors to the apostles. They aren't just the preachers of the Gospel. They are a part of the Gospel. When Christ commissioned them to go and make disciples of all nations (see Matthew 28:18-20), they received Christ's own authority to do so. That authority guarantees the truth of the Gospel being preached.

The Pope, as the successor to Peter, is part of the Gospel in the same way. He is the chief pastor, the chief evangelizer of God's people. But his authority is as much a part of the Gospel as it is a means of preaching the Gospel. Christ's choice of Peter to lead the apostles wasn't insignificant or temporary. It was a deliberate act to guarantee the authenticity of how the Gospel is preached, witnessed, and interpreted until the end of time.

The Church and the World

At the end of His time on earth, Christ told His apostles to "go and make disciples of all nations." He told them to evangelize. That was their primary mission, and it was a mission not limited to one group of people in one time or place. It was a mission for all peoples in all times, and in all places. To make disciples of the nations, Jesus orders the apostles to do so by teaching and baptizing. Here then we see the triple functioning of priesthood—to teach, sanctify, and lead. The apostles are given the charge as well as the power (*potestas sacra*) to carry on the mission of Christ.

That mission is still the primary mission of the Church. The Church offers to the world a personal encounter with Christ. She offers this in her every action—in her preaching, in her sacraments, in her works of mercy. Accordingly, no aspect of the Church is incidental or unimportant—not the way she celebrates her liturgies, not the way she administers herself internally, not even the way she has the floors of her buildings swept. Everything matters because everything is a part of how she manifests Christ to the world.

The world, of course, matters too. The Church can't limit her activities or the work of evangelization to the realm of doctrine and worship. Man lives in society. He images God as a lover, a creator, and a thinker in society. He finds his vocation in society (EN 49–50).

As such, the Church has to concern herself with culture and with those living outside the Church. The truth and the gifts she possesses aren't simply for the faithful. They're for the whole world. And what she has to offer is not simply religious truth or religious wisdom. Rather she offers the world truth and wisdom for every aspect of human life— for how we are to eat and drink, work and play, dress and love. That is why the Church talks about marriage, about bioethics, and about art. She is supposed to talk about all the things that make up human life. It's a central part of her mission in the world, and the work of evangelization must include helping people living in the world to live more authentically human lives, lives that reflect who we are and what we're called to be.

And so, any initiative of evangelization must consider how the Church herself is a part of the message. She not only preaches the Gospel of Christ, but she also preaches who she is—indeed, the Body of Christ. Parishes need not be bashful or ashamed of their apostolic character, their Catholic identity, the unity and holiness they possess. So often the passivity of preaching the Gospel of Christ results in a fear of not wanting to offend someone or to be so inclusive that the "mystery" of the Church is lost to all the garble of inclusive language. If evangelization is going to be effective, the Church cannot have an identity crisis. She is Christ incarnate, and that is a gift to the world today!

One of the challenges in evangelization is our need for the Church. The independent mindset of so many leaves people with a spiritual crisis of wanting to believe in God without the Church. "Me and my Jesus" is often the mantra of those who are convinced they can be Christians without the burden of belonging to the Church. Christianity is reduced to living an ethical life, being a nice person, possessing a so-called spirituality of praising the Lord, but doing so on my terms. The evangelizer is challenged by these sentiments and obviously needs to live the faith as one who loves the Church.

This is something I often had to address strongly with seminarians. You must love your bishop, you must love your own diocesan church, and you must understand that the normative experience of "Church" for Catholics is through their parishes. In the communication age even faithful Catholics can undermine the efforts of the Church when bishops are attacked or ignored, or when people see their membership in the Church as relating solely to the universal Church and not to the diocesan Church and their parish as well.

Similarly, evangelization is challenged with a pluralism among those who do see the importance of community, but who seek it in another denomination where one feels more welcomed, where the celebration of worship is more entertaining, or the minister simply preaches better. The evangelizer must convince the believer that the one, holy, catholic, and apostolic Church completely subsists in the Catholic Church and, while we do not always live out what God has blessed us with, the Church herself is indefectible and will always possess everything that Christ has given to her.

The Anthropological Foundation of Evangelization

No one can escape the Gospel. We can try. We can close our ears to truth and allow our eyes to be blinded by sin. We can deny truth and reason. We can deny Revelation. In this life, God permits people to walk away, forbidding the Church to impose the Gospel on anybody. No one can be forced to believe.

But eventually, in the next life if not this one, we all have to reckon with the Gospel. And that's because the Gospel is what reveals our ultimate destiny. The Gospel, and only the Gospel, possesses the answer to man's perennial question, "Why do I exist."

The answer to that question is the fourth foundation of evangelization, the anthropological foundation.

The anthropological foundation of evangelization tells us that the Gospel isn't just about God. It's also about us. And because the mystery of our existence unfolds in the Gospel of Christ, the work of evangelization includes presenting the fullness of that mystery. It also includes taking that mystery into account in the methods, as well as the message, of evangelization.

The mystery that the anthropological foundation of evangelization presents is this: Man is made in the image and likeness of God. That's what sets him apart from the rest of creation. He is, in fact, the sum of creation, what everything adds up to, the what and the why of it all. The world is his home. It was created for him to inhabit. It was also created to reveal God to him. And it was created so that he could image and serve God in his work—caring for creation, shaping it, and offering it back to God in worship and sacrifice.

When sin entered into the world, however, it marred man's likeness to God, as well as his relationship to the world. The Gospel tells us this. But it also tells us that through the saving mysteries of Christ, man's image and likeness to God can be restored. Christ paid a heavy price to restore the dignity of creation. By entering into a relationship with

Christ through His Church, man can recover his created dignity. He also can receive supernatural dignity.

The fact that we are creatures, created beings, the handiwork of another, is an important part of our coming to see this. If we can recognize that we are creatures, then we can also come to know that there is a Creator. If we can recognize that there are limits on what we can do or make happen, then we can come to recognize our dependence on another.

Of course, even when we recognize that, like dogs, cats, tulips, and clouds, we are created, the work of another, we can also recognize that we are different from everything else we encounter in the world. We are living, breathing beings, capable of doing great good and causing great harm. We love, we think, we build, and we create. And most of all, we long for something. We look beyond ourselves for answers to why the world is broken. We look for truth. We look for a kind of lasting happiness that our reason should tell us not to expect on this earth.

The fact that every human being has the capability of "believing" and that all men desire truth and happiness beckons the question: Is there an ultimate truth, an ultimate happiness, something ultimate to believe in? Philosophically speaking, the fact that all men of all times possess these desires must mean that something ultimate is waiting for us. For example, hunger and thirst, something we all experience, can be satisfied with food and water. The desire to be loved is satisfied by a parent, friend, or family member. So, the desire for an ultimate truth, happiness, and belief must mean these realities exist. And, of course, they do.

What we look for is God.

That search reveals that even though we are creatures, we are nonetheless called to transcendence. We're destined not only for a natural end, but for a supernatural one. We're destined for God.

Authentic evangelization urges men to pursue all that is truly human—music and art, literature and science, work and family life—because all those experiences are avenues of truth. They lead us to God. But authentic evangelization also insists that none of those things, in and of themselves, can fulfill the quest each of us is on. We cannot lead a truly human life unless we're also pursuing a relationship with God.

Absent Him, our lives will always be less than they should be, because a relationship with Him is our ultimate goal and our ultimate destiny.

When the Church proclaims the Gospel, she proclaims something that people want to hear, whether they recognize it at first or not. She doesn't just proclaim a list of doctrinal beliefs we're called to profess. She proclaims that for which our hearts long—the truth about God, the truth about man, and the truth about the world.

Faith and Conversion

That truth, however, comes with demands. The anthropological foundation of evangelization tells us that the goal of evangelization is not for us to simply hear truth and give intellectual assent to it. God doesn't just want our heads; He wants our hearts. That's why evangelization seeks to transform our hearts first and then, through that transformation, transform the heart of society. That's also why faith requires that we do more than accept doctrines about who Jesus Christ is. It requires that we accept what He preached about how man is called to live. It requires that we order our lives accordingly. It requires that we bring every moment of our day and every aspect of our life into conformity with the Gospel. And it requires an inner transformation and the unending conformation of our lives to Jesus' life. That is the substance of conversion, and conversion is exactly what evangelization seeks to bring about (EN 23).

Think about how love changes the lives of that newly married couple; think about how hope spurs that young person to dream and pursue his goals; think about how the entrepreneur takes risk for the value of success. People change their lives when affected by the experiences of love, hope, and success. So it is with faith. When we strategize and determine how we will make the Gospel of Christ effective, what we are considering is how the lives of people can be changed when faith is embraced.

Finally, the anthropological foundation of evangelization recognizes that we help people understand that conversion is not merely a private matter between them and God. Faith and conversion should lead us into the community of believers. There, we find more than mere fellowship.

We find the means to grow in our faith and experience ongoing conversion. The Old Testament reveals the will of God that people are "chosen" to be a part of a community where believers will celebrate together what God has given to them. The Church, the eschatological community that transcends boundaries of time and space, is comprised of believers who also celebrate together and, in doing so, continue to experience ongoing conversion and a deepening of faith that could never occur without the Church, the Body of Christ. By receiving the sacraments, hearing the Word of God, serving others, learning more about the faith, and growing in our prayer lives, we become more and more the image of God we're called to be. Through the work of evangelization, we become truly and fully human.

***

In whatever age the Church exists and in whatever place she seeks to proclaim the Gospel, these four foundations of evangelization hold:

1. God wills that all men be saved.
2. Christ reveals God's will and accomplishes it.
3. The Church proclaims what Christ revealed and accomplished and helps all men to enter into the saving mysteries.
4. The Gospel is the answer to men's deepest desires and can bring about their inner and outer transformation by drawing them into communion with other believers in the Church.

The world has changed since the time of Christ; the world has changed since the time of the 1974 Synod of Bishops. Yet, these four foundations haven't changed. This is what we are to teach and why we teach it. To proclaim the Gospel is to proclaim these truths. This is the substance of evangelization. And as we move forward into a new age, carrying out a new evangelization, these four foundations must remain the four cornerstones of all our efforts. Neglect one, and no matter what we try to build, it will crumble.

This is what we call "theological pluralism"—when these four foundations are compromised. For example, all people desire to be saved (soteriological) but may reject Christ as the one and only savior. Or, one may accept Christ as Lord and Savior (christological) but may reject the Church as the means to experience Our Lord. One may acknowledge that happiness and truth are the goals of human life, but may not see God as the source of this pursuit.

Evangelization must be a complete experience for both the believer who is sharing his faith with others and the "hearer" who is listening to this proclamation. Because our American tradition allows for a pluralism in how we pursue the American dream (which is a good thing), the way we live our faith as Catholics can often be compromised with the mindset that "everything is up for grabs as long as I am a good person who doesn't hurt anyone else." Unfortunately, the result is a Gospel not totally preached or lived, and certainly a very limited experience of who Jesus is.

CHAPTER 3

The Here and the Now:

The Essentials of the New Evangelization

The starting point for defining the new evangelization is the ending point of the 1974 Synod of Bishops on evangelization: Man. One could conclude that the Synod of Bishops was reclaiming the overall ecclesial nature of evangelization: The Church exists in order to evangelize. With the rapid growth of progress in some parts of the world, the destruction of societies in other parts, mankind is living through an era where so many are enslaved—either to the materialism of success or to the poverty of societal neglect. Pope John Paul II's call for a new evangelization and Pope Benedict XVI's continuance of that call leads us to a somewhat more anthropological nature of evangelization: Man exists in order to be evangelized. Man exists so that he might hear the Gospel, discover God, and fall in love. *We* exist because of God's love and for God's love.

That truth reminds us why we evangelize, and it reminds us why the world needs us to evangelize. Every man, woman, and child on this earth needs Christ desperately. Apart from Him, we can never know who we really are. Without Him, a question mark hangs over the meaning of our life. When we are evangelized, however, the deepest longings of our hearts are fulfilled. And when we evangelize, we help others find that same fulfillment, that same joy. In calling for a new evangelization, John Paul II called the Church to renew and redouble her efforts to lead the world to joy. That's not proselytizing. That's love.

So, what does this love look like in action? What defines it? What does it seek? The "new evangelization" is the key for anyone involved in ministry today. One cannot effectively be involved with the Church's mission without understanding the impetus for the new evangelization that John Paul II and Benedict XVI have called the Church to embrace.

There is not a priest who can effectively carry out his ministry without comprehending what this new evangelization entails.

Neither John Paul II nor Benedict XVI has given us any one encyclical, letter, or any other singular statement that answers all questions about how to do evangelization. Since John Paul II first used the words "new evangelization" in a 1979 homily in Poland, the term itself has developed and evolved. But that doesn't mean the new evangelization can't be defined, or that it doesn't have clearly identified goals. It can and it does.

Defining the New Evangelization

In 1979, Pope John Paul II told his fellow Poles that "a new evangelization has begun." But it wasn't until four years later, in Haiti, that he actually called for a new evangelization for the entire Church. There, in an address to the Latin American bishops, he said that what South America needed was not "a re-evangelization," but a "new evangelization, new in it its ardor, method, and expression."[1] The Holy Father was beginning to recognize new pastoral situations in which Catholics were leaving the Church for other denominations which seemingly were promising something better. In other parts of the world, Catholics were not stepping up to the plate to combat immorality. They were simply silent. Still others were choosing to not even have their children baptized. All of these situations require the Church to seek a "new evangelization" that brings the Good News to people in a more effective manner.

The phrase, "new in its ardor, method, and expression," is crucial to understanding the new evangelization. The new evangelization seeks newness in its methods, not in its message. It looks at the world and says, "This place isn't what it used to be." It recognizes what modernity and post-modernism have done to men, and admits that if the Church wants to reach people, it has to do things a bit differently. Essentially, the new evangelization says that the Church doesn't evangelize in a vacuum: She evangelizes in a culture, and that culture has to be taken

---

[1] Pope John Paul II, Opening Address of the 6th General Assembly of CELAM (Latin American Episcopal Council), (March 9, 1983, Port-au-Prince, Haiti), *L'Osservatore Romano* 16/780 (April 18, 1983): 9.

into account when she carries out her mission of proclaiming Christ. For the Church in America, that means, as Pope Benedict told the U.S. bishops during his 2008 visit to Washington, DC, "recapturing the Catholic vision of reality and presenting it in an engaging and imaginative way to a society which markets any number of recipes for human fulfillment."[2]

All those "recipes," of course, have been strongly flavored by a flawed understanding of man. Our political, social, and economic systems— systems which modernity and post-modernism produced—enslave man while claiming to liberate him. They make him less important than the system, and have taught him that happiness and truth can only be attained through things, that God has nothing to do with happiness or truth. The new evangelization, on the other hand, seeks to humanize and Christianize the culture so that man can fully and freely pursue a relationship with God and find the end God has for him. When we talk about a new evangelization, we're not talking about a shift in the criteria of evangelization, but rather a shift in how we evangelize primarily seeing culture as the venue by which man develops, lives, and grows. Since the conditions in which we live are always changing and new, the way the Church carries out her evangelical mission also needs to be new.

Again, that doesn't mean what she proclaims changes. The new evangelization doesn't water down the Gospel or its demands. The four foundations of evangelization still hold. Rather, the new evangelization emphasizes a starting point that considers the culture of man and how that culture can benefit man. The Gospel of Christ is what brings true freedom and happiness. Therefore, the Church seeks to promote an authentic humanism that guarantees freedom for all.

A Call to All

And it is all men and women that the new evangelization seeks to reach. When John Paul II first spoke of a new evangelization, he identified three distinct groups in need of evangelization: the unbaptized who live

2 Pope Benedict XVI, Address to U.S. Bishops at the National Shrine of the Immaculate Conception (April 16, 2008). Available at http://www.vatican.va/holy_father/benedict_xvi/speeches/2008/april/documents/hf_ben-xvi_spe_20080416_response-bishops_en.html

in communities that have never heard the Gospel; the baptized who believe and practice their faith, and therefore need ongoing conversion; and the baptized or children of the baptized who have fallen away from the Church and lost a sense of living faith.

Initially, the pope applied the term "new evangelization" only to the Church's outreach to that last group—lapsed Catholics. He spoke of the Church's evangelical activity to the baptized as "the pastoral care of the faithful," and its missionary activity to the unbaptized in the traditional terminology of *ad gentes*, "to the nations." This division existed, at least in part, because of practical pastoral priorities. It was the old Gospel adage, "You are the salt of the earth; but if the salt loses its flavor how shall it be seasoned?" (Matt. 5:13). John Paul II believed the Church first needed to revitalize the faith in previously Christian countries so they could then bear witness to the rest of the world.[3]

At the end of the last millennium, however, John Paul II expanded the use of the term "new evangelization" to apply to the Church's outreach to all three groups: the unbaptized, the practicing baptized, and the non-practicing baptized. In *Ecclesia in America*, he wrote:

> As I have said on other occasions, the new and unique situation in which the world and the Church find themselves at the threshold of the Third Millennium, and the urgent needs which result, means that the mission of evangelization today calls for a new program which can be defined overall as a new evangelization.[4]

In other words, the new evangelization was no longer considered just a part of the Church's evangelical efforts or just another evangelical activity *within* the Church's mission, but rather *the* evangelical activity of the Church. This understanding of the new evangelization still holds today. It is how the Church understands her call to preach Christ to the

---

[3] Pope John Paul II, Apostolic Exhortation on the Vocation and the Mission of the Lay Faithful in the Church *Christifidelis Laici* (December 30, 1988), nos. 34–36.

[4] Pope John Paul II, Apostolic Exhortation on the Encounter with the Living Jesus Christ: The Way to Conversion, Communion, and Solidarity in America *Ecclesia in America* (January 22, 1999), no. 66.

baptized and the unbaptized, the believing and the unbelieving. All of us need Christ and His Church, just as all of us live in a culture awash with obstacles to grace. The same things that prevent the unbaptized from hearing the Gospel and the same things that lead Catholics away from the faith—the culture's temptations to unbelief, immorality, and radical individualism—also present serious challenges to those trying to live out their faith. The new evangelization takes these obstacles into account in its presentation of the Gospel, using a new language and new methods of witnessing to lead all men to what John Paul II called "a fresh encounter with Jesus Christ." Now we also see how Pope Benedict XVI is asking the Church to reclaim the mystery and awe of our faith as a direct way to evangelize culture. An important component of the success of the new evangelization is indeed to reclaim the wonderful traditions that have directly influenced music, art, literature, science, architecture, and even political systems. Each generation certainly has much to offer in shaping the culture. Yet to purge society of Christian values and traditions only serves to undermine the dignity of mankind.

The Church's Mission in the Modern World

The new evangelization is more than just a new language. It is, in many ways, the ongoing implementation of the Second Vatican Council.

When John Paul II initially called for a new evangelization, he didn't intend a break with the vision of evangelization set forth by the Second Vatican Council or by Pope Paul VI's *Evangelii Nuntiandi*. Rather, he intended the new evangelization to carry that vision forward into the new millennium, writing in *Tertio Millennio Adveniente*: "The best preparation for the new millennium . . . can only be expressed in a renewed commitment *to apply*, as faithfully as possible, the teachings of Vatican II."[5]

John Paul II saw the Council, with its call for the Church to enter into culture and engage culture, as the catalyst for spiritual renewal in the Church. He also saw it as the Church's interpretive guide for understanding its mission in the modern world. For John Paul II, Vatican II

---

[5] Pope John Paul II, Apostolic Letter on Preparation for the Jubilee of the Year 2000 *Tertio Millennio Adveniente* (November 10, 1994), no. 20 (emphasis in original).

was the mother of the new evangelization, giving birth to the concept and guiding it with her vision of man, the Church, and the world. That's why we can speak of the new evangelization as an expression of the Church's mission in the modern world. [6]

We can also think of it this way: The Church has not only survived two thousand years worth of man-eating lions, sword-wielding fanatics, and lawsuit-filing attorneys, she has thrived. She has grown from a tiny band of Jewish fisherman to a worldwide family. She has carried out her Master's commission to preach the Gospel to all nations. And she owes her success to God's grace. But that grace didn't just open people's minds and hearts. It taught the Church how to speak, how to preach, and how to witness to the Gospel in different places and times. The Spirit is always creative, never stagnant, which is why the Church is always young at heart. She always must renew herself from within, remaking herself more and more into the image of Christ, so that she can be His voice in the world. Finding new ways to speak and new ways to witness is her ever-present task. The new evangelization is how she does that today.

In the new evangelization, however, the Church does more than speak. She also walks. The new evangelization is as much about the Church walking beside man as he journeys through this life, as it is about telling him where to go. As the Body of Christ, the Church bears the responsibility for showing the world Christ's love, Christ's mercy, and Christ's wisdom. She calls man to repentance and conversion, and supports him as he repents and converts. She supplies answers for his questions and comfort for his sorrows. This is why Pope John Paul II called the Church an expert of humanity in his first encyclical, Redemptor Hominis ("The Redeemer of Man"), for indeed she is. The Gospel is meant for everyone—even those who will not profess faith in Christ or His Church, the truth that emanates from the Gospel can still shape the cultures of man. The Church has something to offer even to non-believers. This really is the impetus of the new evangelization: dialoguing with culture. Purifying culture of everything not intended by God is a goal of the new evangelization. The result of a successful

---

[6]   Pope John Paul II, *Tertio Millennio Adveniente,* no 20.

evangelization is a person who is living a more fully human life, living in freedom and in truth.

Given the culture in which we live, doing that isn't always easy. Instead of being cynical or preaching a doomsday message both John Paul II and Benedict XVI have urged the faithful to see these conditions as an opportunity—an opportunity to preach the Gospel, to witness with our words and lives to the truth of what we believe. Modernity and post-modernism, with all the violence, alienation, and sorrow they have produced, have also produced the conditions for what John Paul II called "a new missionary age."[7] Because of the conditions of today, people are seeking and searching for spiritual fulfillment. This is good. The Church, embracing this sense of a new evangelization, needs to know how to respond to this yearning. In the early centuries of the Church heresies required the Church to define very clearly in what it is the Christian believes. Similarly, the spiritual yearning of our people today requires the Church to use a language and a method which elicits a response in which people experience Jesus Christ, who is our Lord and Savior.

The state of the world today has separated so many people from the source of meaning and happiness that the emptiness inside them grows harder and harder to ignore. The world is ripe for conversion, and the new evangelization calls us to seize this moment.

What the New Evangelization Is Not

Like many of the Church's terms that often get bandied about, the term "new evangelization" is often misused and misunderstood. Topping the list of misunderstandings is the idea that the new evangelization, in some way, is a new Gospel.

It's not.

Again, the new evangelization is about methods, not the message. If it were a new message, it wouldn't be evangelization at all—at least not the sort of evangelization Christ intended when He commissioned His apostles to preach the Gospel to all nations. The new evangelization cannot present a new Gospel because the Gospel is unchanging. The

---

[7] Pope John Paul II, Encyclical Letter on the Permanent Validity of the Church's Missionary Mandate *Redemptoris Missio* (December 7, 1990), no. 92.

Gospel is not a package of ideas developed by men and focus-tested for their effectiveness and marketability. It's truth—God's truth. Accordingly, the Gospel message itself can't be adapted for different people living in different cultures in different times. It doesn't seek to make itself palatable or compatible with ideologies and philosophies *du jour*. The Gospel simply is, and man can choose to accept it or reject it, not modify it.

Accordingly, the new evangelization seeks to present the truth about God and man in all its fullness. The four foundations of evangelization emphasized by the 1974 Synod of Bishops and by Pope Paul VI in *Evangelii Nuntiandi* remain with the new evangelization: God wills that all men be saved; salvation comes through Christ, who is God made man; the Church is the means through which men enter into the saving mysteries of Christ; life with Christ is the destiny for which all men long and for which all men were made.

The new evangelization does not give credence to current theologies that attempt to strip Christ of His divinity and present Him either as a self-help guru or as a radical revolutionary whose message has warped through the centuries. It also does not nod in agreement with modern and post-modern misconceptions of freedom that set man up as the arbiter of his own truth and separate religion from the rest of life. "Freedom is not an opting out," Pope Benedict has explained. "It is an opting in—a participation in Being itself. Hence authentic freedom can never be attained by turning away from God."[8]

Just as the new evangelization doesn't seek to present a new Gospel, it also doesn't seek to restore some past Catholic golden age. "It is not a program for the so-called 'restoration' of a Europe of former times," John Paul II explained in a 1991 synod. Rather, he continued, the new evangelization "helps to uncover [culture's] Christian roots and to build a more profound civilization, clearly more Christian and therefore more richly human."[9]

---

[8] Pope Benedict XVI, Address to Catholic Educators, Catholic University of America (April 17, 2008). Available at http://ewtn.com/library/PAPALDOC/b16uscathed.htm.

[9] Synod of Roman Catholic bishops from the Atlantic to the Urals, "Declaration of the Special Synod Assembly for Europe" (December 13, 1991), no. 3.

Simply put, the new evangelization does not try to take the Church and the world back to 1950, 1350, or 250. It is not about reproducing the past. It's about rehabilitating man, about helping him recover his authentic dignity as the image and likeness of God.

In order to do that, however, the new evangelization does look back to the past to retain what is truly "human" and what "culture" is really about. It doesn't dismiss what's old as useless or irrelevant simply because it's old. It recognizes that Catholics in the past knew a thing or two that could help us today. Those are the transcendentals—truths about men, God, and culture, as well as pious ways of expressing those truths that are universally true for all men in all times. The new evangelization seeks to recover these transcendentals. It looks for what Pope Benedict XVI has called the "continuous interweaving of the divine and human in the life and history of people," and uses what it finds in the creation of a new Christian culture.[10]

The new evangelization also seeks to retrieve from history the same sense of inspiration and commitment that motivated Christians through the centuries. In doing so, John Paul II explained, the Church attempts to help all her children navigate through the changing times in which we live. Connected to the unchanging faith of the Church, we can live the Gospel today with hope for living the Gospel tomorrow. Through the new evangelization, the Church reassures us that we don't have to fear living "in a period of passing from one shore to another."[11] The Kingdom of God is always at hand.

A third misconception about the new evangelization is that the phrase is interchangeable with the word "re-evangelization."

In his initial call for a new evangelization, John Paul II explicitly stated that the Church needed a commitment "not to a re-evangelization, but to a new evangelization." That is because re-evangelization is not possible.

When we are evangelized and accept the Gospel or when our parents commit to raising us according to the Gospel in the Church, the

---

[10] Pope Benedict XVI, Address at the Conclusion of the Vatican Museum's Fifth Centenary (December 16, 2006).

[11] Pontifical Work for Ecclesiastical Vocations, *New Vocations for a New Europe:* Final Document of the Congress on Vocations to the Priesthood and to Consecrated Life in Europe (January 6, 1998), no. 12.

Church marks us with the sign of Baptism. That sign is a real sign, forever stamping our soul. After Baptism, evangelization doesn't cease. It continues as a process of ongoing conversion. That process may or may not continue to unfold in our life. We can reject, dismiss, or drift away from the faith. But we cannot rid ourselves of the mark of our Baptism. Nothing we do can remove it.

No one can be re-evangelized, because no one can be re-baptized. Faith can be renewed or revitalized. Separated sheep can return to the fold. But there are no "do-overs" when it comes to valid Baptisms. The term re-evangelization implies otherwise, which is why we should avoid it and never confuse it with the new evangelization. Sometimes we see other denominations employing the notion that Catholics have not been saved and therefore will "re-baptize." To re-awaken the faith and speed that person along the road of conversion is a dimension of this new evangelization. As the bishops of Latin America wrote:

> To speak of a new evangelization does not mean that the previous one was invalid, sterile, or short-lived. . . . The expression "new evangelization" does not mean re-evangelizing . . . as though there were no first evangelization but, rather, to start from the many rich values it has left in place and proceed to complement them by correcting previous shortcomings.[12]

So it is the first evangelization that in fact makes the new evangelization possible. The work of the new evangelization uses the remnants of the first—the inclinations to virtue, embedded values, and ways of thinking that the faith gave to individuals and cultures—to call people to the faith and to a deeper life of faith.

When parishes begin to strategize about pastoral priorities, they must consider how to best reach those Catholics who have drifted away and how to continue feeding active Catholics. Meeting people where they are and then encouraging them to embrace the Cross, in whatever

---

[12] CELAM (Latin American Episcopal Council), *Santo Domingo Conclusions: New Evangelization, Human Development, and Christian Culture* from Fourth General Conference of the Latin American Bishops (October 12-28, 1992).

form it is taking in their lives, becomes the saving message of the Gospel and the mission of the Church.

The Goals of the New Evangelization

Thus far, we've talked about what the new evangelization is and what it is not. What we haven't talked about is what this new evangelization should do for the Church and the culture. What do we expect to come of it? What end are we after? What's the point of it all?

The point is to vanquish secular humanism from the culture and build a new culture rooted in Christian humanism.

The end result of modernity and post-modernism is secular humanism, a way of seeing the world that distorts how we understand ourselves, the way we are to live, and even why we live in the first place. It claims to put man at the center, to make man's happiness and freedom the goal of all the culture does, but because it leaves God out of the equation entirely, it ends up harming man more than helping him. It leads men away from God, and the longer it governs the culture, the harder it becomes for men to find God and lead lives worthy of His call.

The "humanism" that culture promotes is not entirely misguided— the advances of science, medicine, and technology to sustain the dignity of human life are admirable. The "secular" pursuit of this humanism is what concerns the Church because the very success that humanism seeks to achieve ends up marginalizing groups of people or even takes their lives away.

The new evangelization is a response to secular humanism. It recognizes the damage done by it to all those living in contemporary culture and looks for new ways to reach damaged hearts and minds with the truth of Christ. Its end game is to unmask the devilry of secular humanism, undo the damage done by it, and give rise to a different kind of culture altogether, a culture governed by Christian humanism.

Like secular humanism, Christian humanism places man at the center of creation. But unlike secular humanism, man is the center of creation because God has placed him there for the purpose of preparing mankind for the heavenly Kingdom. Christian humanism promotes an authentic development of culture in which all peoples discover their vocation in life without being suppressed from the so-called "freedom" that secular humanism promises. It recognizes the Gospel in all its fullness, and it gives man the freedom to pursue truth by giving him a culture that recognizes the real meaning of freedom and the sacredness of life. It makes it possible for men to find God, love God, and do all that He calls them to do.

Christian humanism approaches the cultures of our world as civilizations of love. Purifying culture from all sin and evil permits man to see, experience, and enjoy the presence of God's Kingdom. Thus, even the non-Christian can see the benefit of the Church's mission because the Church is not seeking to proselytize people into believing what they may not yet be prepared to accept. Rather, the Church proposes and incarnates the Gospel of Life into the realm of culture. The moral norms of the Gospel are not sectarian. One does not need to profess their faith in Jesus Christ to recognize the moral norms of human life. The new evangelization allows the Church to dialogue with the agents of culture to promote what is truly human. To accomplish this ultimate goal, however, the new evangelization requires Christians to embrace three other goals in their mission as disciples: holiness, communion, and the manifestation of the Kingdom of God.

The Call to Holiness

A culture formed by Christian humanism can only arise when those of us living in the culture strive to be holy—to love God with all our hearts and minds, and to love our neighbors as ourselves. That's why the new evangelization calls us to conversion. Every person is ultimately a religious being—God has implanted in each of us the desire for truth. Since God has placed this appetite within us, only He can satisfy the hungers of our soul. The supreme vocation for every human being therefore is holiness—to be perfect as our heavenly Father is perfect, to allow God's grace to consume us. Without God's grace, our appetite is fed from only what the world can give, thereby poisoning our soul or at least denying us the full potential of life lived as God intended. We have a lot of unhappy people because they have sought only what the world can offer. Holiness is the result of God's grace filling our souls with love. Everyone is called to holiness.

Helping people answer the universal call to holiness begins with helping them recognize that such a call exists. God doesn't only call priests and nuns to holiness. He also calls electricians and accountants and even theologians to holiness. Conversion is the action that gets us there. It is a continual turning away from self and turning toward God, seeking His will, His mind, His love. As a process, not a one-time act, conversion comes about only through the grace of God by the action of the Holy Spirit. But it can't happen at all unless people know that it's supposed to happen. The Church has been given the mission by Christ to baptize all peoples and teach all nations the Good News. That knowledge necessarily precedes conversion and discipleship. The Church is therefore restless: We disciples are not satisfied until people around us truly know who Christ is and how the Church mediates the grace of God in what she has been given by Word and Sacrament.

Once people freely accept the call to holiness, surrendering them-selves to God and becoming disciples, the Church then bears the responsibility for helping them grow in faith. Her mission is to pass on all the means God has entrusted to her for helping people enter into His saving mysteries: the liturgy, the Scriptures, the Church's doctrinal teachings, the sacraments, acts of piety and devotion, prayer, and spiritual direction. Those of us on the receiving end of these gifts, namely all believers, have a responsibility as well. We are called to practice our faith in complete obedience, accepting the gifts of the Holy Spirit, using them to grow in the life of grace and, in turn, sharing our faith with others.

The thrust of the new evangelization charges all those belonging to the Church to be more deliberate, purposeful, and committed to clearly sharing the Gospel with others. "In the uncertainty of this time in history and of our society, offer people the certainty of the complete faith of the Church," urged Pope Benedict soon after the beginning of his pontificate.[13]

---

[13] Pope Benedict XVI, Address to Austrian Bishops' Conference on the occasion of their *ad limina* visit to Rome (November 5, 2005). Available at http://ewtn.com/library/PAPALDOC/b16austria.htm.

To do that, we must hand on the ancient traditions and mysteries with integrity, fidelity, and joy, and in new and fresh ways, using new words, new avenues, and new methods to teach ancient and unchanging truths. The new evangelization doesn't call us to abandon older forms of piety, such as the Rosary, Benediction, or Eucharistic adoration. It also doesn't call us to abandon teachings difficult for contemporary culture to swallow—the evils of abortion and contraception, the sacredness of the marital act, or the existence of the Last Things: death, judgment, heaven and hell. And it most definitely does not call us to jettison or water down the sacraments—to downplay the necessity of Confession, the importance of receiving the Eucharist worthily, or the lasting, binding nature of marriage.

All that *was* still *is*. We just have to help people with minds scarred by secular humanism to understand those truths and embrace them. How well we do that is what will either help people fall more deeply in love with God and attain real holiness, or lead them to fall away from Him into nothingness.

Creating Communion

God is a family, a communion of three Persons giving themselves to one another in love. Man, made in God's image, longs for that same experience of communion. Each of us longs for friendship, for love, for community. Spouses, children, friends, and co-workers fulfill that long-ing to a certain extent, but they can't fulfill it entirely. That's because our supernatural longing for communion runs deeper than our natural longing. The natural longings, in fact, only point the way to the supernatural one, and only a relationship with Christ can fulfill that longing. Again, we understand that God has implanted this hunger into our souls; we are thirsting for a real sense of communion. Evangelization is not concerned about creating in man a need for communion, for that need already exists. Rather, evangelization responds to that supernatural longing by drawing believers together into a community that Christ inaugurated at the Last Supper—"do this in memory of me."

The Church, as Christ's Body on earth, gives all believers a real experience of supernatural communion. She gives us Christ in the Eucharist and she gives us a foretaste of heaven, when all the saints gather around God's altar. She helps forge in the here and now the supernatural bonds of unity that will reach their fullness in heaven.

Those bonds are attractive and powerful. People want them, and the possibility of attaining them is a compelling reason to enter into the life of the Church. That's why *communio*, the communion of believers in the life of grace, is an effective source of evangelization. When we show the world what the communion of faith looks like, we are showing them a glimpse of God Himself. For when we are gathered, He is with us. Like the song exclaims, "they will know we are Christians by our love" —our love for one another and our love for God. When we live the law of love, we give people a compelling reason to believe and to reorder their lives around the Gospel.

Creating an authentic Christian humanism, a civilization of love, requires that the Church visibly and clearly manifests *communio*. "Contemporary society is questioning and observing the Church, demanding consistency and daring in the faith," Pope Benedict reminded us.[14] I sometimes think American Catholics are bashful about wanting others to see how we function as a faith community. We are still influenced by the thinking that our relationship with God is only personal and private. Maybe our spirituality has a personal component, but our relationship with God is a communal event. When the world sees us gathered by the millions with our Holy Father, when a city sees thousands of people gathered with their bishop, when a local community sees hundreds of people gathered with their pastor, when a platoon sees a few soldiers with their chaplain, when the inmates see other inmates at Sunday Mass—what is seen is a community gathered by God. There is no other experience of *communio* that the world could possible ever offer.

---

[14] Pope Benedict XVI, Address to Bishops of Northwest Mexico during their *ad limina* visit to Rome (September 8, 2005). Available at http://www.catholicculture.org/culture/library/view.cfm?recnum=6630.

In order for the Church to fulfill her mission, the unity we profess as one Church we must also guard. The unity of the Church is what Christ prayed for and what God expects. The Church needs every aspect of her life to point to communion and unity. This unity needs to shine forth from episcopal conferences and bishops, dioceses and parishes. It also needs to shine forth from the faithful's adherence to the deposit of faith handed on by the college of bishops under the authority of the successor of Peter. In other words, bishops need to teach the same truths consistently, priests need to preach the same truths consistently, and lay people need to profess the same truths consistently. Unity is not manifested by ecclesial infighting or cafeteria Catholicism, the picking and choosing of which doctrines and virtues people find convenient to their needs or compatible with their lifestyles.

Unity, of course, doesn't mean uniformity. The Church's diversity and the diversity of her members help the world understand what *communio* means. Black and white, charismatic and traditionalist, English-speaking and Spanish-speaking, Opus Dei and Communion and Liberation, all have a place in the Body of Christ, and all make the Body richer and fuller because of their unique contributions. That diversity reveals *communio* as a possibility for all men and women of all stripes when grace is present and guiding. When the rest of the world witnesses that phenomenon, the Gospel comes alive.

Building the Kingdom of God

The Kingdom of God is where the call to holiness leads us. It is also where *communio* becomes a visible, palpable reality. It was preached by Christ in His life on earth, inaugurated by Christ in the paschal mystery, and is ruled for all eternity by Christ in heaven. He is the King of the Kingdom, and His subjects are those who repent, believe, and live out their repentance and belief by practicing justice, mercy, and charity.

The Church, as the Body of Christ, is inseparable from the King and His Kingdom. She is, in fact, the sacrament of the Kingdom, the visible sign of the Kingdom on earth. She is also the guardian of the laws and values of the Kingdom—she knows what will make man happy, what true justice and freedom are. Those laws and values are the laws and values of authentic humanism. They are the foundation for the culture that the new evangelization seeks to build. The Church indeed is an expert in humanity, as John Paul II once wrote, in light of her travels through time, dialogue with culture, and confrontation with sin.

When they ask what the purpose of the Church is, evangelization ought to convince people that the Church herself is not the goal of her mission; rather, she is a sign that points to the Kingdom. She is a sacrament of the Kingdom, making it present by the culture of faith that she is. In order to build that culture, however, the Church first has to model it. She has to show the world what a civilization of love looks like.

At the time of the 1974 Synod of Bishops, confusion existed about the extent of the Church's mission as it relates to the political forces that were undermining the freedom of people, as is still the case today. The social teachings of the Church make clear not only how the Gospel, when lived in its totality, eradicates the social sins of man such as discrimination, racism, inequality, etc., but also assures that the Church, as the Body of Christ, manifests the Kingdom of God. She is not a merely human institution that is responding to various social situations. Many of the interventions by bishops at the 1974 Synod called upon the Church to be more effective in bringing the Gospel of Life to societies that were being destroyed by Marxism, communism, and materialism. However, the means to preach this Gospel could not and cannot be worldly, political, and certainly not imposed or forced as some camps were proposing.

The Church has always seen herself as the champion of the poor, the little, and the weak. She has to urge individuals and states to protect and strengthen families, to empower communities on the local level, and to respect in every word and deed the dignity of the human person. Above all, she must clearly and consistently defend the right to life as the most basic, most fundamental principle of any just society. "It is by respecting the human person that peace can be promoted," Pope Benedict said. "And it is by building peace that the foundations of an authentic integral humanism are laid."[15]

---

[15] Pope Benedict XVI, Annual Papal Address to the Diplomatic Corps Accredited to the Holy See "Preaching the Gospel, Serving Humanity, and Building Peace" (January 8, 2007). Available at http://ewtn.com/library/PAPALDOC/b16diplom07.htm.

The Church illuminates the nature of rights and freedom with the Gospel, helping people understand political, philosophical, and social questions in light of the truth about man and God. To do this, she draws on her own vast resources of wisdom about the nature of justice and charity, questions of war and peace, and the relationship of individuals to governments, employers to employees, families to society, and the wealthy to the poor. By imparting this wisdom to the faithful and culture, she doesn't so much offer the world specific solutions to specific problems as she offers guiding principles by which specific solutions can be found. Proclaiming these principles, the principles of the Kingdom, is a necessary part of supplanting secular humanism with Christian humanism.

It's not enough, of course, for the Church to just preach these values. She also has to live them. As Pope Benedict told the Pontifical Academy of the Sciences, "The responsibility of Christians to work for peace and justice, their irrevocable commitment to build up the common good, is inseparable from their mission to proclaim the gift of eternal life to which God has called every man and woman."[16] The proclamation of John the Baptist confirmed by Jesus Christ is that the Kingdom of God is at hand. Working to manifest this Kingdom is working to overcome all that impedes the Kingdom, which means defending the rights of all people, eradicating poverty, discrimination, and racism, and promoting a culture of life where all have the right to live.

That's why the new evangelization so strongly emphasizes the principle of solidarity—the Church walking with the world in its struggles—urging all believers to help the world confront the challenges it faces today, challenges ranging from pornography to healthcare, the environment, divorce, the push for same-sex marriages, corruption, and AIDS.

While John Paul II stressed that the Church is called to be more than a social services agency, he also urged dioceses and parishes to

---

[16] Pope Benedict XVI, Address to the Participants in the 14th Session of the Pontifical Academy of Social Sciences (May 3, 2008). Available at http://www.vatican.va/holy_father/benedict_xvi/speeches/2008/may/documents/hf_ben-xvi_spe_20080503_social-sciences_en.html.

commit financial and human resources to confronting these challenges.[17] By feeding the poor, caring for the sick, and protesting injustice we evangelize ourselves, learning more about who we're called to be. We learn by doing. We build up the Kingdom of God from within and we make it clear to the rest of the world what the Kingdom of God looks like, what the Kingdom of God is. We give the world compelling signs of its power and its glory. And by doing all that, we move closer and closer to the day when a civilization of love will rule the earth.

***

In calling for a new evangelization, Pope John Paul II recognized that the Church needed to find a new way of proclaiming the Gospel to people who saw the world through the lens of modernity and post-modernism. He knew we needed to devise new ways of doing old things—calling people to repent, to believe, to love. In the years since John Paul II's death, Pope Benedict XVI has repeated that call, urging the Church on all levels to address the problems the world faces now in a language contemporary people understand. One question, however, still remains.

How?

---

[17] Pope John Paul II, Apostolic Exhortation on Jesus Christ the Savior and His Mission of Love and Service in Asia: ". . . That They May Have Life, and Have It Abundantly" (Jn. 10:10) *Ecclesia in Asia* (November 6, 1999), no. 24. Available at http://www.vatican.va/holy_father/john_paul_ii/apost_exhortations/documents/hf_jp-ii_exh_06111999_ecclesia-in-asia_en.html.

PART III

The How

CHAPTER 4

The Means and the Method:

Hinges of the New Evangelization

I wrote at the outset of this book that there is no one program for carrying out the new evangelization. The new evangelization, like evangelization itself, is a mystery. It will unfold in different places in different times with different people in different ways. It's flexible, adaptive. It can't be put into a box.

But, again like evangelization itself, certain unchanging elements guide it. These include the four foundations of evangelization: the soteriological, christological, ecclesiological, and anthropological dimensions of mission. Those foundations express the language of the new evangelization and the theological realities underlying it. There are also, however, methods that make for an effective evangelization. It is my contention that for evangelization to be successful there are two hinges on which any process moves: inculturation and catechesis.

Inculturation and catechesis are the "how" of the new evangelization. They are how the Church is to preach Christ in the here and now. Just as modernity and post-modernism are the hinges upon which our culture turns, so inculturation and catechesis are the hinges of the new evangelization.

Giving the Word Flesh

Inculturation is a relatively new entry in the Church's lexicon. It was used at a 1959 conference in Louvain, Belgium, that focused on the Church's mission in non-Christian cultures.[1] Then the term meant something a little different than it does today. It described the process

---

[1] See Mariasusai Dhavamony, *Christian Theology of Inculturation* (Rome: Editrice Pontificia Universita Gregoriana, 1997). Dhavamony cites *Mission et cultures non-chrétiennes* (Louvain: Desclee De Brouwer, 1960).

of inserting the Gospel into a culture after the culture was disposed and prepared to receive the Good News.

In the 1960s, the word appeared here and there in the occasional theological journal. The bishops did not use the word directly but spoke of methods during the 1974 Synod of Bishops. However, the Synod prepared the Church, soon after, to adopt the concept "inculturation" in a theological sense. Inculturation was subsequently the subject of an intervention at the 1977 Synod of Bishops, which addressed catechesis, and also of a letter the Superior of the Jesuits sent to all his priests in 1978. In both cases, inculturation was identified as a method of evangelization. Not until John Paul II released *Catechesi Tradendae* (the apostolic exhortation resulting from the 1977 Synod of Bishops) did any pope use the word, and even then its meaning was still loose and undefined, with John Paul II using "inculturation" and "acculturation" interchangeably.

Soon, however, the term took on its definite and current form, passing from neologism to an essential method of the new evangelization, with John Paul II saying in 1992:

> [Remember] the inherent missionary nature of the Church means testifying essentially to the fact that the task of inculturation, as an integral dissemination of the Gospel and its consequent translation into thought and life, continues today and represents the heart, the means, and the goal of the new evangelization.[2]

The dissemination of the Gospel and its translation into thought and life—that's the essence of inculturation. Inculturation is incarnating the Gospel in culture, giving it flesh in the language, signs, and symbols of a particular people in a particular time and place. As new as the term may be, the meaning of it, the act of it, is as old as the Gospel itself. And that is because inculturation is simply allowing the Word of God to be experienced in a practical way. The *way* God makes His Word present is the basis for understanding inculturation from a theological standpoint.

---

[2] Pope John Paul II, Address to the International Council for Catechesis "Gospel Meant for Every Culture" (September 26, 1992).

Mirroring the Incarnation

Long before the coming of Christ, God spoke to men, Hebrew men, in their own language, explaining Himself through the signs and symbols of their culture. He communicated His Word to them, teaching them how to live, love, and worship. Then, in God's good time, His Word became flesh.

Jesus Christ was born in a specific culture to a specific woman in a specific family. That family professed Judaism as their faith. Their community was oppressed by a specific leader, Herod, and a specific people, the Romans. Jesus adopted a profession; He became a carpenter, like His foster-father Joseph. And when He began His ministry, all those realities—His experience and the background of those to whom He spoke—formed His preaching. Their faith traditions, their economic and political struggles, their habits of eating, drinking, working, resting, celebrating, and mourning are all realities that influenced how Jesus would carry out His mission of redemption and salvation.

When Jesus died, He died a death specific to His time and place—crucifixion. Later, when Christ's apostles began carrying out His commission to make disciples of all nations, they did so in the same manner as their master: preaching the Gospel using the language, symbols, and signs of their culture. They talked about the Law, about ritual, about poverty-stricken widows and temples to unknown gods. They drew on all that surrounded them, all that the people understood, to make their message known. And as people heard the Gospel, it took a definite shape in the lives of those who embraced it. It became incarnated in their thoughts, their speech, and their daily habits of living. They cared for widows and orphans, dealt honestly with their neighbors, and gathered on the Lord's Day to celebrate the Body and Blood of Christ.

What God did before and during the time of Christ prefigured how the Church would carry out her mission after Christ returned to the Father. From the time of the apostles until now, the Church has incarnated the Gospel into cultures. She has revealed the power of God's love through her liturgy, sacraments, doctrine, and pastoral care, preaching with authority, forgiving with certainty, and loving all men equally. She has founded universities, erected cathedrals, and created art that gives form to the stories of salvation history. She also has transformed pagan feasts into Christian holy days and absorbed tribal rituals into her catalogue of traditions. She has disseminated the writings of the Fathers, translated the Scriptures, and canonized the holy men and women of villages, cities, and nations. She has done all this in such a way that the Gospel has come alive in specific cultural contexts.

Today, as always, the Church is the sacrament through which Christ makes Himself present in culture. It is her sacred duty to continue until the end of time what God initiated at the beginning of time. She preaches the Gospel so that it can take flesh in our world. She makes concrete the mysteries of Christ—His life, death, and Resurrection—so that those mysteries can become concrete in our lives, in the decisions we make, in our conversations, our spending habits, our work, our treatment of others, in the way we vote, the way we dress, and even the way we eat. Through this, she accomplishes the goals of the new evangelization: She helps us answer the call to holiness, create communion, and build the Kingdom of God.

To do that, however, those of us who are charged with preaching and teaching the faith have to proclaim the Gospel in ways that are rooted in the concrete experiences of people's lives. We can call this an "inculturated evangelization." Like Christ and the apostles, the words we speak, the stories we tell, the examples we give, the relationships we build, the communication tools we use, all have to spring forth from the time and place in which we live. They have to mean something to people. They have to be capable of speaking to people. They have to take into account what people think, value, and want. Again, that doesn't mean that we *adapt* the Gospel to culture. Rather, it means that the Church discerns the values of that culture which are consistent with the Gospel and use those aspects as a bridge or an entry point for the rest of the Gospel.

When it comes to inculturating the Gospel in America today, we must take into account the influence of modernity and post-modernism, as well as the founding principles of American society—the inalienable rights and liberties afforded to every human person.

In more practical terms, that means an inculturated evangelization that confronts the lies that poison the culture—the primacy of science over faith, the nature of progress, the rejection of the wisdom of the past, and the relativity of truth.

It also means helping people think about the true nature of rights and freedoms—their source and their purpose—as well as the true nature of happiness.

It means appealing to their desire for God and for community, showing them how the Gospel counters the loneliness and alienation produced by modernity and post-modernism.

It means helping them channel their desire to do good and give back, using service projects and mission trips to form those who serve.

It means taking into account their distrust of authority, the weight they give to personal experience, and the importance of personal witness.

It means remembering that Americans are consumers who will base many decisions about the faith on the benefits it will bring to them.

It means recognizing that most Americans will not sit down and read the *Summa* when they want to know more about the faith, but rather will look to the same sources of information that they look to for information about everything else in their world—namely, the Internet.

It means using the latest and best resources that have been given to us to teach the faith, especially the *Catechism of the Catholic Church*.

It means providing Catholic alternatives to cultural markers such as books, music, movies, and even T-shirts.

An inculturated evangelization in American culture makes the Word of God alive in such a way that Americans recognize it as a real saving force. The Church—from diocesan programming to individual parishes—becomes familiar with culture without ever identifying with it since the Gospel can never be isolated to one particular culture. Inculturating the Gospel in contemporary American culture means coming to understand where people are today, what matters to them, what they long for and struggle with, and then using that understanding as a way of introducing them to the Good News.

Inculturation through Interculturation

An inculturated evangelization shapes the way the Gospel is preached. That process, however, requires both dialogue within the Church and dialogue between the culture and the Church. As stated before, inculturation does not mean that we adapt the Gospel to fit into one particular culture. While culture can influence the means by which the Gospel will be preached, culture does not shape or form the Gospel. It is the other way around—the Gospel is meant to share the culture in which man lives, in which he develops as a person. A successful inculturation of the Gospel therefore requires what can be understood as "interculturation" —the dialogue between faith and culture.

Man cannot develop, grow, or even discover his vocation without culture. Culture indeed is a reality within creation that God intends. Culture is good. It is required. However, culture is incomplete. The Genesis account reminds us that God calls us to be agents of creation and culture, forming it with values we discover. In short, culture needs the Gospel of Christ to complete it. The way man lives his faith will shape culture into something beautiful, unique, and reflective of God's Kingdom here on earth.

The Church, as a sacrament of the Kingdom here on earth, is also a society ordered as the Body of Christ. Like any society, the Church possesses structure, a language, customs and rituals, laws, community, and tradition. Just as Jesus Christ, the Son of God, interacted and dialogued with the culture of His time, so too does the Church dialogue as one culture to another. Interculturation allows the Church to share what she has with the cultures of the world, and for the cultures of the world to share who they are with the Church.

The premise for evangelization is that God ordains "culture" as the means for man to grow. The Church therefore needs to truly study and become aware of that culture in order for the Gospel to be a protagonist in the development of that culture. So often people see the Church as an enemy of culture, when in fact she is its greatest friend. Interculturation can occur when the culture of the Church magnifies more effectively what has already been established in a particular culture. The Church brings her history, customs, liturgy, theology, and community to culture, raising it even more to greatness. Likewise, culture then allows the Gospel to be understood and lived from the unique experience of that culture, showing the rest of the world another way in which this timeless, unchanging Gospel can be lived.

Having said this, society, which is the product of man's attempt to support the particular culture, can begin poisoning culture with permissiveness or an oppression that purports to be an agent of culture. Since the Gospel is a universal, transcendental truth for all men and all ages, the Church is able to preach this Gospel when society attempts to ruin culture. When the Church speaks out on a developed country's attempts to impose abortion and birth control laws on a developing country, that's interculturation. When the Church condemns a country's unethical economic practices, that too is interculturation. Through interculturation, at the very least, a culture learns some of what the Church teaches and the Church grows in her understanding of how that culture thinks. She learns more about what she must say and do to speak truth to that people. At the very best, the culture imbibes what is universally true so that truth can take on its own unique expression in that culture, becoming more fully what God intends for it to be.

Interculturation takes place within the Church as well as without. This happens when different ecclesial communities learn new ways of preaching and celebrating the Gospel from each other, enabling them to influence, stimulate, and assist one another in carrying out the Church's mission. It also ensures unity between particular Churches and the universal Church, keeping individual dioceses on the same page as the Magisterium and not allowing any one particular Church to isolate itself in a ghetto of its own making.

That's why we have bishops' conferences, synods, encyclicals, and a multitude of other types of communication within the Church. The Church in Peoria learns from the Church in Denver about better ways to conduct the RCIA process. The Church in England learns from the Church in the United States about how to assimilate immigrants. The Churches of France, Belgium, Portugal, and Denmark learn from the Church in Rome about the importance of conducting the liturgy according to the mind of the Church. Through all this sharing and learning, the various parts of the body strengthen one another, enabling the work of inculturated evangelization to remain fresh and relevant, while at the same time, unchanging.

Faith and Culture

As noted earlier, underlying both inculturation and interculturation is the importance of culture to the transmission of faith. Culture is not something apart from God and His plan. In fact, culture has an especially important place in God's plan for the world, because, as *Gaudium et Spes* states, men and women "can achieve true and full humanity only by means of culture."[3]

Cardinal Joseph Ratzinger, now Pope Benedict XVI, once wrote that without culture we are left with a "naked faith."[4] The truth that faith reveals to us comes from God, but the experience of truth, in faith, requires matter. Language, signs and symbols, art and music—all those things give form to faith. Faith needs culture to express itself. It needs culture to express the living, tangible truths of divine Revelation. Culture, in turn, needs faith.

At its best, governed by the truths and virtues that come from faith, culture can enable us to be all that God created us to be, giving us the conditions we need to freely answer His call and discover the meaning of our existence. At its worst, infected by our own sin, culture can lead us away from God, away from truth, away from meaning.

Human activity gives birth to culture, but culture is more than a human activity. Our very nature demands that we need each other and live in harmony with each other. Because God gave us that nature, culture was always part of God's plan for men. He intended culture to be the means through which His truth took flesh in our daily lives. He intended culture to convey and reflect the transcendent.

Accordingly, because we are creatures of both matter and spirit, culture should reflect both the material and spiritual aspects of our

---

3 Second Vatican Council, Pastoral Constitution on the Church in the Modern World *Gaudium et Spes* (December 7, 1965), no. 53.

4 Joseph Cardinal Ratzinger, "In the Encounter of Christianity and Religions: Syncretism is Not the Goal," *L'Osservatore Romano* English edition (April 26, 1995): 5–8.

existence. It should touch on the work we do, the food we eat, the clothes we wear, the houses we build, and all the other physical details of our existence. But it should also connect all those physical details to spiritual truths—the truth about man and the truth about God. Every genuine culture should reflect an impulse each of us carries deep within, a yearning for the transcendent. It should be open to God and His Revelation.

So what does all this have to do with inculturation and the new evangelization?

Everything!

First, by recognizing that culture is part of God's design, intended to help man on his journey to God, we can see how critical it is to incarnate faith in culture. Separation of Church and State is not the same thing as the separation of faith and culture. Faith needs culture. Culture needs faith. We can't just let the culture in which we live go its own way, racing away from God and truth. The Church is a part of that culture. It's the air we breathe, the language we speak, the path we walk. Try as we might, we cannot separate ourselves from culture. We might be able to minimize some of its influence on us by curtailing our exposure to certain elements within it—watching less television, spending less time at the mall, homeschooling children or sending them to solid Catholic schools—but we cannot shake its influence entirely. Nor can we abandon it to its own fate.

Second, by recognizing that culture arises from human activity and is free to develop according to its own principles, we can see that we don't have to try and fit American culture into some prefabricated mold. A culture governed by Christian humanism in twenty-first century America does not and should not look like a culture governed by Christian humanism in twenty-first century Africa or, for that matter, thirteenth-century Italy. And in our work of preaching the Gospel and incarnating the Gospel we shouldn't try to destroy that which is uniquely twenty-first century American simply because it is twenty-first century American and not thirteenth-century Italian.

Just as every human being in some wondrous way uniquely images God, so too does every culture possess the inherent ability, in some wondrous way, to uniquely image God. In the work of evangelization, inculturation helps us discern what in a culture is compatible with the Gospel, what can be used to present the Gospel, and what can help the Gospel flourish. An inculturated evangelization calls us to keep and use the good, jettison the bad, and purify the whole, so that the culture can be, again, what God intends for it to be.

Giving Men Life

The new evangelization uses the method of interculturation to incarnate the Gospel into culture and thus provides a lived experience of how Christians can bring about the Kingdom of God in their own particular circumstances. The second hinge of the new evangelization is *catechesis*. Catechesis, like inculturation, is nothing new to the Church. The Church has been catechizing the faithful—instructing them and drawing them into the mysteries of the faith—for two thousand years now. Catechesis is and always has been one of her most fundamental duties. *"Go and teach all nations, baptizing them"*[5] —this is the mandate given by Christ to the Church through the apostles. Teaching the faith does have historical influences on the methods we employ to teach. The past twenty years, however, have seen a transformation in how the Church understands catechesis and how she carries out that responsibility.

The fathers of Vatican II recognized that, in our complex and sometimes volatile world, the Church's ability to preach the Good News, to evangelize, depends in large part on the formation and education of the faithful. In other words, the Council fathers knew that the Church needs her laity, as well as her priests and religious, preaching and witnessing to the Gospel wherever they are and in whatever circumstances. Neither the laity nor priests and religious can do that, however, unless they themselves know the faith and have been transformed by it. Accordingly, the Second Vatican Council called for a renewed emphasis on formation as part of the Church's evangelistic efforts.

Like many things called for by the Council, however, it took a little while for everyone to get on the same page about what that forma-

---

[5] See Matthew 28:19-20.

tion entailed, where it fit into the process of evangelization, and what its ultimate aims are. Throughout the 1970s, words like "education," "religious education," and "catechesis" were used interchangeably. At times, catechesis was equated with evangelization. At other times, the two were considered distinct activities, with evangelization subjugated to catechesis or catechesis understood as the fulfillment of evangelization. Then there were the unending debates over the proper content and methods of catechesis, not to mention the seemingly unending experiments with it. It was, in sum, a bit of a mess.

Much of that changed in 1979, when Pope John Paul II released *Catechesi Tradendae* ("Catechesis in Our Time"), the apostolic exhortation issued in the wake of the 1977 synod on catechesis. In it, John Paul II clarified both the unique purpose of catechesis and its relationship with evangelization, giving us an understanding of catechesis that still holds true today.

To Know Christ Jesus

That understanding, in its most basic form, is this: Catechesis teaches people *about* Christ so that they can have a relationship *with* Christ. It provides information that leads beyond knowledge to love. More than a human endeavor, catechesis manifests to believers the eternal truths of God, truths communicated to the Church by Jesus Christ. It aims to develop the initial faith of the believer, to nourish the Christian life of the faithful, and to help the believer understand the mysteries of Christ. In this way, the Word that initially moves hearts and minds becomes understood, accepted, professed, and embraced. It becomes part of a person's being, renewing and transforming his life.

The process by which this takes place should not be merely off the cuff. *Catechesi Tradendae* made it clear that catechesis needs to be systematic and programmed to reach a specific goal. It also has to deal with the essentials of the faith, not with disputed questions of theological research or exegesis. This is because catechesis is not theology. Theology is the study of God. It seeks deeper understanding of the truths of divine Revelation. Catechesis is the act or the process by which the Church hands on those truths and leads people into a relationship with Christ. Theology is the handmaid of catechesis. It serves catechesis. Its conclusions help us understand the content of catechesis. But it is not catechesis.

That doesn't mean, John Paul II stressed, that catechesis shouldn't go beyond the *kerygma*, the initial proclamation of the faith. Catechesis needs to be complete, helping the believer come to know and understand all that the Church teaches about who she is, who God is, and the relationship of man to both. Catechesis must also help people understand how those teachings should affect the way they live each day—what their duties as Catholics are, what their state in life demands of them, and all the other ways in which the faith should inform their decisions and actions.[6]

Although catechesis is its own enterprise, distinct from religious education and evangelization, it can't be understood apart from evangelization. Catechesis is, John Paul II emphasized, a moment within evangelization. He explained further:

Within the whole process of evangelization, the aim of catechesis is to be the teaching and maturation stage, that is to say, the period in which the Christian, having accepted by faith the person of Jesus Christ as the one Lord and having given Him complete adherence by sincere conversion of heart, endeavors to know better this Jesus to whom he has entrusted himself: to know His "mystery," the kingdom of God proclaimed by Him, the requirements and promises contained in His Gospel message, and the paths that He has laid down for anyone who wishes to follow Him (CT 20).

Catechesis does not, of course, replace evangelization in bringing a believer's faith to maturity. Rather, it draws people deeper into the process of evangelization. Its content, while informative, further propels

---

[6] Pope John Paul II, Apostolic Exhortation on Catechesis in Our Time *Catechesi Tradendae* (October 16, 1979), no. 30 (hereafter cited in text as CT).

believers into a relationship that leads to eternal life. It disposes their hearts and minds to ongoing evangelization, to ongoing conversion. In catechesis, the message of evangelization—the Good News of Jesus Christ—is, "probed unceasingly by reflection and systematic study, by awareness of the repercussions on one's personal life . . . and by inserting it into an organic and harmonious whole, namely, Christian living in society and the world (CT 26)."

Catechesi Tradendae also points out that while catechesis is not typically responsible for the initial awakening of faith, it increasingly needs to be presented in such a way that it can have that effect. After decades of poor catechesis and faith formation, no priest or teacher can ever assume that someone's presence at Mass on Sunday or their involvement in parish ministries means they have been well catechized. Most likely, it's just the opposite (CT 19).

Regardless, even if they know the faith well, even if an almost complete catechetical breakdown had not swept through the Church in America in the years following Vatican II, both the young and the old in the pews would still need catechesis. As Pope John Paul II explained, catechesis is not reserved for the very young or for those seeking to become members of the Church. Catechesis is for all those who need to learn more about their faith and for all those who need to be drawn into a deeper understanding and love of the Church. Catechesis is for children who have not yet been confirmed and for adults who were confirmed forty years ago or more. Catechesis is for parents bringing children into the Church and it is for grandparents mourning their children's absence from the Church. Catechesis is for everyone; it is part of the ordinary life of faith for all believers (CT 18).

And that is because the faith is richer and deeper than what the world's best RCIA program or twelve years of stellar Catholic education can ever completely convey. On-going catechesis of the faithful is always necessary so that the fullness of the faith can unfold in people's understanding and lives. Catechesis is a moment in evangelization, but it is a moment that goes on and on through the years.

So, what does that moment look like in the new evangelization?

Inculturated Catechesis

Catechesis, like evangelization itself, does not take place in a vacuum. It seeks to form the faith and transform the lives of real people with real problems, real fears, and real hopes. Those people live in a specific time and place, and those problems, fears, and hopes are influenced by that time and place, by the culture in which the people live. Evangelizing any group of people requires catechesis. What the new evangelization tells us, however, is that evangelizing any group of people *effectively* requires inculturated catechesis.

Inculturated catechesis, like inculturation itself, takes into account the people, place, and time. It considers who man is and where man is in embracing the Gospel. In America today, it considers all that modernity and post-modernism have taught him about truth, existence, and the state of the world. It also considers all the scraps of knowledge about God and the Church that he has picked up in the course of his life. It then presents the Church's teaching with all of that in mind, but without compromising a single truth about God, the Church, or man.

Inculturated catechesis is also creative and resourceful in how it makes that presentation. It adapts itself to how people learn and where people learn. It adapts itself to the conditions of contemporary life, looking for the best times and places to catechize people plagued by busyness, over-scheduling, and a set of priorities formed more by the culture than the Church. Likewise, it draws methods of presenting the Gospel from the culture itself, looking to the culture for language, signs and symbols, values, and interests that it can use in the work of leading people to Christ.

But while inculturated catechesis is flexible, open to what it can learn from and about the culture, that doesn't mean it isn't systematic. It is. The pedagogies of catechesis present the Gospel in a systemic manner according to how that person is capable of hearing, receiving, and professing their faith in Jesus Christ. Part art, part science, and part mystery, inculturated catechesis looks to three coordinates to help define its nature and responsibilities: orthodoxy, orthopraxy, and culture.

Orthodoxy, to some, is a rather frightening word. They see it as the enemy of freedom and believe that somehow it will stunt or prevent a creative catechesis that prepares the believer to truly live his faith in the world. That, however, is nonsense. A person can't live their faith unless they know their faith. Watering it down, leaving inconvenient bits out, or letting disputed bits in serves no one. It doesn't get the people being catechized or those doing the catechizing any closer to God. And getting closer to God is *the* point of catechesis.

If we are going to lead people to God, we must lead them along the right path, the one established by God and entrusted to the Church. That path is made up of sacred truths—truths that form the content of catechesis—and those truths are not ours to fiddle with. If we do, the end result will be something shallow, hollow, and superficial. It will not be a living faith, a faith that transforms. And it will certainly not be a faith capable of meeting the challenges presented by our contemporary culture. An inculturated catechesis is, first and foremost, an orthodox catechesis.

The bishops of the United States have taken this dimension of their ministry seriously. Shortly after the promulgation of the *Catechism of the Catholic Church* they formed an ad hoc committee that would assure that all catechetical materials used in the classroom were in conformity with the *Catechism*. People have a right to know that what and how they are being taught is in accord with the mind of the Church. As a result of the ad hoc committee, bishops were able to identify a number of catechetical deficiencies in the texts being used to catechize children. Many of those resources have been corrected and today children are being better catechized. The efforts of the bishops were not to stifle the pedagogies used in catechizing children but, rather, to enhance those methods that guaranteed a complete presentation of the Gospel with age-appropriate material.

This brings us to the second coordinate of inculturated catechesis: orthopraxis. The Good News, given by Christ to the apostles, is the content of catechesis and the source of all catechetical endeavors. It is never enough, however, for the Church to just preach the Good News. She has to preach it in such a way that the message is actually heard and received. That is where orthopraxis comes in.

Orthopraxis demands a pedagogy, a method of teaching, that considers where believers are, what speaks to them, and what can be used to lead them to a deeper union with Christ. God has always communicated His will to us in a way that we can understand. He has made His Word accessible and understandable, and we have to do the same in handing on that Word. At times, this can mean altering or adapting our language to meet the needs of the faithful.

Small children and teenagers, the Appalachian poor, and the denizens of the Upper East Side may all speak English, but they don't necessarily speak the same language. Without abandoning an inch of content or compromising the authentic meaning of a single term, the orthopraxis of catechesis always keeps the various ages and groupings of the faithful in mind when determining which words and methodologies to use in preaching the Gospel.

Orthopraxis also emphasizes the passing on of the Church's social teaching. It forms consciences, so that the faithful can live their faith, not just know their faith. It is attuned to the culture, cares about the culture, and prepares people to transform the culture. That is why the bishops of the United States prepared and released a catechism for adults in the United States that takes the catechesis of the universal catechism and presents it according to the needs and mindset of American Catholics. When the Gospel is lived in force, peoples' lives are changed and their relationship with Jesus Christ shines forth. The beneficiary of such faith is a culture renewed by the lives of Catholics who are manifesting the Kingdom of God in what they say and do.

This leads to the third coordinate of inculturated catechesis: culture. Inculturated catechesis uses culture to transform culture. It draws on a culture's language, values, and expressions to offer culture what it was always meant to have: Christ and the transcendent. It also considers, as one of its most fundamental tasks, the formation of the faithful as evangelizers of culture.

In *Evangelium Vitae* ("The Gospel of Life") Pope John Paul II decried the number of Christians who don't connect the truths they claim to profess with the way they live their lives. How, he asked, can the Church be a credible witness to the truth, when those who claim to believe in that truth contradict it in some of their most fundamental actions? In other words, why on earth would anyone believe that Christ, His grace, and the sacraments could fulfill the deepest longings of their being and lead them to eternal joy, when Catholics lie, cheat, malign, and abuse their bodies (and feel all the more miserable for it) at just about the same rate as the rest of the population? Or Catholics who have political, juridical, or legislative positions in society failing to bring the universal truths of the Gospel into those spheres because they feel those truths could offend someone else?

An inculturated catechesis seeks to transform hearts as well as minds. It helps people see the connection between what they profess in the Creed on Sunday and how they act Monday through Saturday. The relationship we have as Catholics with Jesus Christ is more than a doctrinal relationship—it is personal. Catechesis helps us to bring that relationship into the culture in which we live because the Gospel of Christ is meant for everyone. Even those who will not profess faith in Christ or His Church benefit from the truths that emanate from the Gospel. The Catholic faith is to move beyond the walls of the local parish church and affect its surroundings. Catechesis draws us into a deeper knowledge of Christ and the Church so that we are confident in bringing our faith to others.

If catechesis is truly to influence society, shepherds must be capable of communicating the Gospel. Parents must live their faith as Catholics and as Americans. Catechists, catechetical administrators, and school teachers need to see faith as an integral part of society and, then, teach that faith, preparing young people to be patriots and disciples without confusion or conflict.

Lived Reality

What does all that demand in practical terms?

First and foremost, it demands well-formed priests and well-trained catechists. It demands that the people preaching and teaching know their stuff and know how to present it. That is why the Church has placed an increased emphasis on fixing some of the academic and formational deficiencies in U.S. seminaries in recent years. This is also why, again and again, the U.S. Bishops have called on parishes to make the hiring and retention of highly trained directors of religious education and adult faith formation a budget priority.

It also demands looking for every opportunity possible to catechize people—from parish work days and movie nights to Sunday homilies and cable television shows—not simply limiting catechesis to evening formation classes.

It demands incorporating different teaching methods, recognizing and accommodating different learning styles, and using various teaching tools, such as visual, audio, and discussion-based resources, to get the Gospel message across.

It demands solid resources—well-written and faithful textbooks, Bible studies, and formation programs—that counter popular misconceptions about the nature of God, truth, the Church, human nature, and more.

It demands connecting the unchanging truths of the faith to the way we live now—helping people see what the nature of the Trinity has to do with their marriage, what the Eucharist has to do with the way they eat, or what the evangelical counsels have to do with the way they spend their paycheck.

And it demands addressing people's felt needs and concerns, using their struggles and questions about things such as parenting, finances, relationships, and aging as opportunities for formation.

That, of course, is just the beginning. Different parishes, age groups, ethnic communities, and economic brackets all come with different demands. That, however, is the whole point of inculturated catechesis. It takes those demands into account, adjusting and adapting to what works best in each community.

Inculturation and catechesis are the hinges of the new evangelization. Upon them, the whole enterprise turns. Inculturation gives the Good News flesh. Catechesis hands on the content of the Good News so that it can give life. Inculturation and catechesis are the means by which the Church brings the Gospel to culture and transforms culture. They are how a true Christian humanism can come into full flower. At least, they are how a true Christian humanism can flower in theory. But what about in reality? What do inculturation and an inculturated catechesis look like in practice?

CHAPTER 5

From Theory to Reality:

The New Evangelization in Practice

Thus far, we've dealt mostly with theories and theology. Now, it's time to get practical. Theories are necessary. They inform our thoughts, guide our actions, and aid our judgment. We cannot live without them. Structures, processes, and planning all rely on theory. But, as important as theories are, we don't live in theory. We live in reality. And reality is multi-dimensional. It's filled with matter. It's messy. Nobody knows this better than a good priest or catechist. Experience has taught us that imparting the faith isn't simply a matter of standing in front of people and giving a solid lecture on Church doctrine. That's usually part of it, of course. We won't get anywhere without giving a good explanation of what the Church teaches. But a straight reading of the *Summa* will not be the singular cause for conversion.

Preaching and teaching the Gospel in reality presents preachers and teachers with two chief challenges. The first is to demonstrate and connect the rich doctrine of the Church to the realities man confronts each day. Jesus Christ showed how one's faith does change the way one thinks, acts, and makes decisions. We need to show people that the Trinity, transubstantiation, reconciliation, and redemption are more than just ideas: They are facts that have a practical effect on each of our lives. They are facts that correspond to felt needs in each of our hearts. And they are facts that demand concrete actions by us. Even more important, we have to show how faith is also more than about facts. It is about a relationship with Jesus Christ. The purpose of evangelization is to invite people into that relationship and then nourish that relationship. If the relationship is missing, everything else we do is in vain.

The second challenge is to help people hear what we're saying. This applies to both the people in the pews and the people in the streets.

More often than not, all the bits and pieces of their own messy realities get in the way of people hearing and immediately accepting the Gospel. Our sins, fears, thoughts, feelings, memories, and hopes, not to mention our cultural conditioning, often prevent our ears from hearing and our eyes from seeing the Truth. Finding a way past all of that is not easy.

But it's also not impossible.

The stories that follow tell of priests and catechists who've done just that, who found a way to help people hear, accept, and embrace the Gospel. They are stories of people who understand the demands of the new evangelization and who are meeting them. They are stories of the new evangelization in action. They are also stories that show the way to inculturate and catechize Americans in the twenty-first century.

Each story gives flesh to a principle that is essential for successfully carrying out the new evangelization. The principles illustrated are not an exhaustive list. Ms. Emily Stimpson, a noted writer for Our Sunday Visitor, provided me these stories in order that I could help articulate what I believe are principles for effective evangelization in our country today.

Love the People You Evangelize

After two years of teaching in Ohio, Amy Roberts returned to her home diocese in Tennessee to begin teaching religion at Knoxville Catholic High School. She was young, inexperienced, and believed she had much to prove. She worried about the students not taking her seriously. She also worried about her fellow teachers not taking her seriously. Going into her first year of teaching in Knoxville, the advice someone once gave her haunted her: You can always lighten up on discipline, but you can never get tougher.

So she started out tough. Very tough. Her guard was up, her personality hidden. All business and no fun, she kept her care and concern for the students carefully hidden. Needless to say, it was a rough year for Roberts. None of the students took advantage of her. But none of the students loved her either, nor did they learn from her like she wanted them to. They knew *about* God and His Church, but they didn't *know* God and His Church.

The first few weeks of her second year at Knoxville Catholic mirrored that first year. Then, Roberts had what she calls a "moment of grace," a moment where she saw herself the way the students saw her—hard and unloving. None of the love that she had for the students was evident to them. They didn't know the delight she took in them, the things she wanted for them, and the things she wanted to give them.

From that point on, Roberts resolved to relax, be real, and let her love for the students show. And that made all the difference. As they came to not just respect her, but also love her, they opened up, trusted her, and finally started seeing her as a living witness to Christ. They saw in her what she talked about in her lectures. They believed her because she was finally believable.

In the years since that "moment of grace," Roberts has watched those first students of hers start up their own Bible studies, work with Mother Teresa's Missionaries of Charity in Calcutta, consider the priesthood, and discern the next step in their lives with God's desires, not just their own, in mind. Other influences besides Roberts—not to mention God's grace—helped get those young people to that point, but had she loved them less, or had she kept that love from them more, her part in their journey would have been negligible.

Saint Thomas Aquinas once advised teachers to "Love your students and love truth." Those words are as important today as ever. Perhaps even more important. When it comes to carrying out the new evangelization, nothing matters more than love. After all, God is Love. We can't proclaim Love without love. And because we are made in God's image, we're made to give and receive love. When someone loves us, we can't help but respond to that. When someone doesn't love us, when charity is lacking, the natural response is not only to close our hearts to them, but also to close our ears to whatever they have to say. Pope Benedict speaks about this strongly in his encyclical *Deus Caritas Est*, particularly in the last section when he challenges us as a Church to be the face of love to an often broken world.

The new evangelization is an attempt to preach the Gospel to people who have grown up without love, or without real love. Most people living in our culture have been offered a host of substitutes disguised as love—lust, greed, guilt-ridden indulgence, and selfish manipulation—but none of those substitutes can fill the need each of us has to give and receive real love. When the Church preaches the Gospel with love, when we really love the people we teach and minister to, we give many of them something they've never had before. Because of the effects of post-modernism, we sometimes approach ministry from a corporate, committee, or organizational standpoint rather than from a person-to-person experience. Indeed, structure is important—as a matter of fact, if charisms are meant to endure they are to be institutionalized, such as Catholic schools, hospitals, apostolates, and the like. Yet, the organized efforts of ministry should not replace the person-to-person dimension in which the power of God's love is experienced firsthand. Often we lose some of our people to denominations who practice the personal dimension of ministry.

Be a Witness

When Eric Westby was a youth minister, he ran many great programs for the teens. He planned prayer meetings and Bible studies, one-on-one mentoring sessions, hours of Eucharistic adoration, and evenings for praise and worship. He also set aside days and evenings just for fun—to break the ice, build relationships, and teach the teens the meaning of true fellowship. The teens responded to Westby. The numbers in his youth group grew. But more important, so did the faith of those teens. The youth groups didn't just get bigger; they went deeper. The programs, by just about every measure, were a success.

But the programs weren't the ultimate reason for Westby's success.

One day, not too long ago, Westby, who now runs the Office of Family Catechesis for the Diocese of Phoenix, was talking with his bishop, the Most Reverend Thomas Olmstead. Bishop Olmstead, looking back on his days as a parish priest, told Westby that when he was a pastor, he wanted one thing for the teens: for them to spend time with couples in strong marriages. "Eric, I hope you know the witness of your married life more than anything else stood out to the teenagers you worked with," the Bishop remarked.

Westby knew at once the bishop was right. As orthodox and engaging as his teaching might have been, his own witness mattered more. The teenagers saw that he practiced what he preached. And they saw that while it wasn't always easy, it delivered results. It bore fruit. Living the faith brought Westby and his family a peace, a joy, and a strength that many of them had never before encountered.

When it comes to successfully carrying out the new evangelization, witness walks hand in hand with love. Whether you're dealing with teens or adults, they want to see two things: (1) that you truly believe what you teach and act according to those beliefs, and (2) that those beliefs and actions make a difference in your own life.

They need to see those things for a host of reasons. Partly because we live in a consumer culture, everyone is selling something, and before we buy, we want to know if the goods are genuine. We also want to know if they will benefit us. That applies to the Catholic faith as much as it does to the Apple iPhone.

Post-modernism has also made witness matter more. When everything is relative, when authority is always to be questioned, experience still holds sway. When people can see that, like them, you've struggled, but that you've found answers and help in those struggles through faith. That provides answers, which even the best apologetics cannot.

Ultimately, however, witness matters to men and women because that's how God made us. He made us to live in community and learn through community. He made us to learn from others. God could have infused His truth directly into our brains, but He didn't. He became man. He lived among us, taught us, and showed us what those teachings meant through the example of His life.

For two thousand years, that's how the faith has been handed on, from person to person. People have seen the transforming power of the faith in their priests and their parents. They've also seen it in the lives of the saints. Today, the breakdown of the traditional family and Catholic culture means that many people can go years, even decades, without encountering someone who truly lives their faith, without encountering a strong Catholic marriage, without knowing what Catholic family life looks like, and without understanding that the faith really does change lives.

As a rector of a seminary, I often reflect with the seminarians on what people want to see in their priests. Witnessing to a happy and holy vocation is what inspires our young people. In my experience as a pastor, I learned that people want to see me be faithful to my ordination promises. I don't have to fake it, act like someone I'm not, or present my priesthood in a way that makes me popular. Instead, people want to see me simply being faithful to my prayer life, preaching what the Gospel demands, and enjoying the gift of priestly celibacy.

The witness of believers is crucial to the new evangelization. In order to live the faith, people first need to see it lived. So, live it. And bring your parishioners and students into contact with others who live it. Use mentor couples in the marriage preparation process. Ask families to get involved with your youth ministry program. Invite devout retirees to work with the RCIA team. Do whatever you can to help people find living, breathing, struggling witnesses to the faith. Let them see how Christ has changed the story of your life, so that they can begin imagining how Christ can change the story of their life. Then send them back out into their homes and communities so that they, in turn, can live the faith in front of others. Create an army of witnesses, and you create an army of evangelizers.

Make the Parish the Curriculum

In 2002, when Father Derek Lappe first arrived at his former parish, St. Thomas Aquinas in Camas, Washington, he found some good things—many strong families and parishioners hungering for a deeper understanding of their faith—and some bad things—problematic catechetical materials, sparsely populated daily Masses, and incessant chattering before Mass.

To correct those problems, Father Lappe didn't try to reinvent the wheel. Instead, he relied on "all the things that once helped build Catholic culture, all the things the Church gives us to transmit the faith."

Within a few months of his arrival, he moved the tabernacle back to the center of the church. Every day, fifteen minutes before Mass started, he entered the sanctuary, knelt down, and prayed, giving a witness of how to prepare for Mass. During the Mass, he delivered homilies with some element of catechesis in it. And he celebrated the Liturgy according to the mind of the Church—with reverence, with the focus on Jesus, and with all the "smells and bells" that have marked Catholic liturgy for centuries.

A remodel of the modern church building—incorporating traditional frescoes, a new crucifix to replace the old "Resurrexifix," votive lights, a marble altar, and a new ambo—also had a place in Father Lappe's faith formation plan. So too did the institution of perpetual Eucharistic adoration and the introduction of liturgical music that conformed to Vatican documents on sacred music.

Along with the liturgical catechesis, Father Lappe worked on getting the parish more involved in the community. He directed five percent of the parish budget to helping the local poor and five more to other charitable causes. He continued and expanded previous apostolates—outreach to the homebound and elderly in nursing homes and multi-pronged pro-life outreaches.

Helping Father Lappe was a team of top-notch catechists and volunteers he recruited to help run the programs. And all their efforts bore fruit. Sunday evening programming for families, Lenten missions, guest lectures, and men's and women's retreats became regular and well-attended events. Attendance at daily Mass rose from eight or nine people to upwards of seventy, while the parish itself grew from 550 families to 750.

And everyone started praying quietly before Mass.

In *Our Hearts Were Burning Within Us*, the U.S. Bishops said that Catholic parishes didn't need to launch a whole new series of programs to teach the faith. They just needed to make the parish the curriculum.[1] That's what Father Lappe did. He brought every aspect of the parish's life into conformity with Church teaching. He presented the fullness of the faith clearly and strongly in the only place and time most of his parishioners were likely to encounter anything that even hinted

---

[1] United States Conference of Catholic Bishops, *Our Hearts Were Burning Within Us* (Washington: USCCB Publishing, 1999), 118.

of Catholicism—Sunday Mass. And he drew on two thousand years' worth of wisdom and tradition to do that.

Lessons learned?

First, beauty matters. A beautiful Church, with a beautiful liturgy and beautiful music, communicates the faith. It shows it to people, makes it visible, in a way that mere words cannot. If the parishioners, when they go to Church, only experience what they experience everywhere else in the culture, and if they have no experience of the transcendent when they enter the church and participate in the Mass, one of the most important catechetical tools we have at our disposal is wasted.

Catechetical homilies also matter. Most of the people sitting in those pews on Sunday will not show up for a Bible study on Wednesday. Most of them won't show up for anything at the parish other than Sunday Mass. This is a priest's chance to teach those people. And they do need teaching. The confusion in catechesis since the Second Vatican Council has left the Church with two whole generations of Catholics who do not know the basics of their faith. They don't know what the Church teaches and why. Many also don't know that they are called to have a passionate, loving relationship with Jesus Christ. In truth, they haven't been evangelized.

Yes, homilies need to break open the Word, but Scripture and Catholic doctrine are not in opposition to each other. Doctrine has its roots in Scripture. Scripture is rendered understandable by doctrine. Since the beginning of his pontificate, Pope Benedict has urged priests to show Catholics the relationship between the two in their homilies. Assessing how to do that better is one of the reasons why he called the 2008 Synod on the Word of God. This is a priority of the Pope and a priority for the new evangelization.

Finally, devotions matter. The Rosary, Eucharistic adoration, Stations of the Cross, and novenas to the saints did not suddenly lose their significance on New Year's Day, 1970. They are, as they have been for centuries, instrumental means of handing on the faith. They are incarnational expressions of love and devotion. They are pious acts that give the faith flesh. They teach in a way that no homily can, and they form Catholic identity in a way that no Bible study can. Helping people dive deep into the ocean of traditional Catholic devotions lost or neglected in recent decades is one of the most important things a parish can do for the new evangelization.

The list of lessons could go on and on, because in the end every aspect of parish life matters. From the way the secretaries in the rectory answer the phone to the catechetical materials used and the acts of service performed in the community, everything the parish does can become a teaching moment, a catechetical moment, an evangelizing moment, if we do it according to the mind of the Church.

It is true that there is a large segment of our people who have been formed with a poor ecclesiology in which their experience of the Church remains in the 1970s. Some of our pastors have this same ecclesiology. Therefore, the younger pastors of our Church, and with them the new generation of Catholics who are seeking orthodox and prayerful parish communities, often feel alienated from those who feel threatened by what is a clear movement of the Holy Spirit. Pope John Paul II and Pope Benedict XVI have clearly embraced and called down this Spirit upon our Church, which is bearing fruit all over the world. Our parishes must not be afraid!

Embrace the New Media

Carson Weber has an undergraduate degree in Information Technology. But Weber's office at the Diocese of Sacramento's chancery is not near the other techies. In fact, Weber doesn't do IT work for the diocese at all. He is, in fact, Director of Evangelization for the diocese. Yes, he has the requisite master's in Theology and Catechetics, and has served time on the parish beat. But one of the main reasons Sacramento hired him was because of that IT degree. They needed someone in his position who knew how to navigate through the world of new media and who understood its power for evangelizing.

The new media—mostly made up of the Internet and its spawn: weblogs, podcasts, virtual communities—is fraught with problems. As Nicholas Carr chronicles in the July 2008 *The Atlantic* article, "Is Google Making Us Stupid?" evidence suggests that too much online reading interferes with our brain's ability to read and think deeply—two "must do's" for fully living the Catholic faith in the twenty-first century. There's also the blogosphere's marked resemblance to a bar, where everyone shouts out opinions and no one moderates the discussion. On the Internet, rumors fly fast and furious. Reliability of information is not guaranteed. The same problems apply to podcasts.

Then there's the problem of virtual community getting in the way of real community—young people (and some not so young) spending more time conversing with people online than in person. Personalities can be invented and reinvented at will. The accountability that comes with one-on-one personal interaction is missing. Detachment—from ourselves, from others, and from the consequences of our actions—creeps in. Again, the new media is fraught with problems.

But it's also full of potential. And like it or not, it's shaping the world in which we live. The old media dinosaurs—newspapers, magazines, and television—now incorporate elements of the new media for sheer survival. Television shows with cult followings have their own podcasts. Newspapers hire popular bloggers to write columns for their print editions, while their print reporters' blog for their online editions. Radio programs host websites where listeners can leave comments and discuss with each other the day's topics. The culture as a whole uses the power of the media—new and old—to get its message out because that's what reaches people. And if the Church wants to get her message out, we need to tap into that same power.

The good news is that there are plenty of terrific apostolates doing just that. Tapes and CDs featuring talks by dynamic Catholic speakers have been around for decades, but Lighthouse Catholic Media has taken that a step further, developing kiosks lined with free CDs that parishes can place near their entry ways. The CDs feature talks by popular speakers such as Scott and Kimberly Hahn, Jeff Cavins, Steve Ray, Father Larry Richards, Father John Corapi, and others. For a culture on the move and in their cars, these CDs give parishes an easy way to help people learn more about their faith and learn it from people with a special gift for talking about the faith.

On the worldwide web, Catholic podcasts like Father Roderick Von Hogen's "Daily Breakfast," and Greg and Jennifer Willets "That

Catholic Show" offer engaging presentations of the faith that can be emailed to everyone in the parish address book. Dozens of Catholic news sites, apologetics sites, and resource hubs abound as well. Directing parishioners to apologetics sites such as catholicanswers.org, Scripture studies such as those found on salvationhistory.com, and Catholic news portals such as zenit.org is as easy as putting up a series of links on the parish website or spotlighting a new faith resource each week in the parish bulletin.

There's also terrific Catholic radio programming (both on satellite radio and the old fashioned kind), as well as television programming, which in many areas is on the air 24-7, announcing the Gospel, answering questions about the faith, and conducting probing interviews with Catholic apologists, intellectuals, and cultural leaders.

Right now, there are more good resources out there than there is space here for me to list them. These resources feature people who are the best at what they do—teaching the faith—and who do it through mediums that reach people where they are: in their cars, on the web, in front of their televisions. These resources also can be distributed at next to no cost by cash-strapped dioceses, parishes, and schools. Getting these resources into the hands of parishioners, however, requires that dioceses, parishes, and schools embrace the new media.

So, how do we do that?

To start with, every parish, school, and apostolate must maintain a user-friendly, up-to-date website. Today, when people want information they go to the Internet. When they go there, whether it's to find out a Mass time, look for events coming up at the parish, or find good resources about the faith, that information needs to be there. No parish, no matter how small, can afford not to have a good website anymore. These days, that's about the same as not having a phone number.

For the really adventurous bishop, priest, or director of religious education, embracing the new media can also mean following in the footsteps of Boston's Cardinal Sean O'Malley, and starting their own blog or turning their Sunday homilies into a podcasts for the web. If a diocese can produce a program for the local public access network, it can make a podcast for its website.

Does the new media have its problems? Yes. But does that mean the Church can't use it to proclaim the faith, teach the faith, and lead people to more resources about the faith? Absolutely not. The new media is the voice of America in the twenty-first century. It's almost the language. A Church that doesn't learn how to speak that language and use it as effectively as the rest of the culture, or even more, will be a Church without a voice. And a Church without a voice is not a Church that can evangelize.

Build Catholic Identity

The front of the t-shirt simply says "Catholic Kung Fu." On the back, there is a little more of an explanation: "Never Attack. Always Defend." In the halls of Bossier City High, situated in Bossier City, Louisiana, you'll see a smattering of these shirts, along with maybe a half-dozen other designs, all clearly identifying their wearer as Catholic, and all featuring some play on words or bit of humor.

Two years ago, however, you would have seen no such thing. The t-shirts are the work of Micah Murphy. Murphy has designed some t-shirts and ordered others, keeping a steady stream of what amounts to advertisements for the Catholic faith popping up in the halls of the town high school. Murphy is not, however, in the t-shirt business. He's actually the youth minister at St. Jude, the local Catholic parish.

St. Jude is part of the Diocese of Shreveport, one of the smallest dioceses in the country with only a total of fifty-three thousand Catholics. It is officially, "mission territory," and in Bossier City, while Catholics are few, Protestants are many. The Protestants also have big money to spend on youth programs. Some have their own bowling alleys. One recently bought a local shopping mall to turn into a youth center. Not surprisingly, Protestant youth programs attract more than their share of Catholic teens, who are more than willing to accompany their Protestant friends to church youth events.

When Murphy first arrived at St. Jude, he knew he needed to find a way to get the Catholic kids to come to Catholic events. He also knew that he could never compete with the Protestant churches on their playing field. The purchase of a bowling alley, let alone a shopping mall, was hardly in his tiny parish's budget.

It didn't take long for Murphy to realize, however, that his biggest obstacle was not the Baptist church up the street. It was the lack of Catholic identity among his teens. Like most post-Vatican II children, they knew nothing of Catholic culture and Catholic traditions. The faith was not the number one priority in most of their homes, and even where it was a priority, the parents more often than not expected the Church to take the lead in teaching it to their children. Functionally that meant their Protestant friends and their Protestant communities played a bigger role in shaping their faith than the Church or their families did.

To counter that problem, Murphy began looking for ways to build Catholic identity among his teens. He wanted to get them to see themselves as Catholic, to understand its importance, and to find ways of expressing that identity in public. The t-shirts were part of that plan. So was helping the kids find music by contemporary Catholic artists. By making what they wore and what they listened to something that was identifiably Catholic, Murphy accomplished two things. He gave the teens something that made them unique, banded them together, and helped them publicly express their Catholicism. He also gave them a way of doing low-pressure evangelization among their peers. They witnessed to the faith simply by showing up at a football game in a Catholic t-shirt—t-shirts that preached some of the Gospel on their own and, more often than not, elicited questions about the faith from non-Catholic teens.

Murphy, of course, has done more than design t-shirts. Two nights a week he does serious catechesis with the teens. On another night of the week, he meets them at a local diner just to talk and hang out. Those evenings ultimately accomplish far more than the t-shirts do. The more the kids learn about their faith, the more passionate they become about it and the more they define themselves by it. But having a way to express that faith, to give it flesh in the language of their culture, the youth culture, helps them hold on to it when it could otherwise conveniently be forgotten.

Teenagers are not the only ones who need that. Most adults in the Church today are Americans or Southerners or lawyers or Steelers fans first, not Catholics first. Catechesis can go a long way towards changing that, but something more is still needed. Faith, you'll remember, is never naked. It needs culture to express itself. It needs signs and symbols to give it flesh.

The Catholic Church in America once had a plethora of those symbols, but most went the way of the 1962 missal. As part of the new evangelization, we need to bring some of those symbols back or find new ones to take their place. These symbols could include keeping works of religious art in the home or statues of Mary in the garden, wearing scapulars or crucifixes around our necks, or simply listening to Catholic radio in the car. It may also mean doing things that set us apart—not eating meat on Fridays, crossing ourselves when we drive past a Catholic church, praying before every meal, even in public.

From a pastor delivering a homily about abstinence from meat on Fridays to the parish selling religious artwork as a fundraiser for the school, parishes can help Catholics discover and recover these little ways of bolstering Catholic identity. Regardless of how each parish does it, part of the new evangelization has to entail bringing back some of the old ways of giving expression to the faith in people's daily lives, as well as finding new ways—like selling t-shirts with "Catholic Kung Fu" written across the front. Again, not only do these bits and pieces of a uniquely Catholic culture help evangelize the Catholics who look at them or wear them, but they also give public expression to the faith in the world. They take the signs and symbols of the faith out of the parish and into the culture. They are a low-cost and low-pressure form of evangelization.

Respect Time

As the Diocese of LaCrosse prepared to launch "Faith Alive," a faith-sharing program designed to offer Catholics opportunities to learn about their faith and talk about it with others, they knew that no matter how good the program was, its success ultimately depended on one thing: scheduling. If the program demanded too much of people's time, if they couldn't fit it into their already jam-packed schedules, it would be over before it began.

How to schedule programs and events may be one of the most pressing questions every parish faces. People say they want Bible studies; they say they want adult education classes; they say they want retreats. And they do. But between work and family and commutes and all the other demands of modern life, they simply don't have time for them. The parish is not the center of a Catholic family's life like it was sixty years ago. In fact, for most parishioners, parish events rank near the bottom of their priority list, somewhere below catching the latest episode of a television show and posting new pictures on their Facebook page.

And it's not just parishioners who are busy. It's catechists and priests as well. Everyone is pressed for time, and when that time is not respected, programs fail, catechists burn out, and priests get overloaded.

So what is a parish to do?

In La Crosse, they opted for scheduling "Faith Alive" meetings once a month for ninety minutes, recognizing that for many a weekly meeting was simply too much. In Phoenix, Arizona, parishes have had the most success with women's Bible studies when they schedule them during the school year, in the morning, and provide childcare. Typically more than a hundred women attend these studies. When scheduling men's events, they more often do retreats that begin on Friday evening after work and end Saturday at noon. Short concentrated events that still leave some of the weekend open seem to draw the largest numbers. Likewise, the Diocese of Harrisburg frequently schedules workshops that run all day on a Saturday, rather than meet for an hour every night of the week. That helps the catechists running the workshop as much as it helps the participants.

The key for many other parishes and dioceses may lie in thinking unconventionally. Is there a central employer—a university, a hospital, a factory—where large numbers of parishioners work? Then why not try sending the director of religious education there at lunchtime for a weekly Bible study or book club meeting? Do all catechists teach religious education classes at the parish on Wednesday? Then how about asking them once a month to stay one more hour on that night for catechist training, rather than expecting them to come back on a different night? Or what about setting up a Bible study program through the parish website that allows parishioners to do the study primarily from their homes?

The busyness of modern life is another argument for using mentor couples in sacramental preparation and follow-up. Because this formation model relies on relationships, not programs, informal events like cookouts and family dinners become occasions for formation. Not everyone can find the time to get to a meeting, but everyone has to eat, making these events more schedule-friendly. The same applies to setting up a kiosk of Catholic CDs in the back of the church. Not everyone can get to a Bible study, but everyone has time to kill in the car while they drive from place to place.

By being flexible, adaptive, and accommodating, we can reach more people more effectively than we have for years. We just have to be willing to do that.

Engage the Whole Family

Put ten directors of religious education in a room, ask them what their biggest source of frustration is, and odds are most of them will say the same thing: "The drop-off mentality." By that, they mean the parental habit of dropping a child off for religious education when it's time for them to receive a sacrament, pulling them out of religious education soon after, and never doing a thing at home to follow up on what the child learned there.

For priests and catechists, that is frustrating on so many levels. It's frustrating to see the sacraments treated like an item on a "to do" list. It's frustrating to see your hard work compromised by what your students learn at home. And it's frustrating to see baptized, confirmed, adult Catholics neglecting their own spiritual well-being.

Rather than seeing the catechesis and sacramental preparation of children as an exercise in frustration, however, some dioceses are learning to see it as an opportunity for getting those fallen away (or falling away) parents back into the fold.

In Pittsburg, Kansas, parishioners at Our Lady of Lourdes Catholic Church have made the Generations in Faith Together (GIFT) program one of the key components of their religious education program. GIFT is a national catechetical program focusing on intergenerational learning and community building.

When Our Lady of Lourdes hosted their first GIFT event on September 8, 2007, nearly six hundred parishioners were there. Seventy were volunteers. The second GIFT event, held near Easter 2008, drew the same number of parishioners and 125 volunteers. Although the measure of success for catechetical programs is never numbers, these numbers were hard for the parish to ignore. Previous events had drawn thirty to forty parishioners—tops. So what got so many people there? In large measure, children.

For weeks, the students in their school and religious education program helped prepare for the event. They drew pictures, rehearsed skits, and learned songs. When those students showed up for the actual event, they brought their parents with them.

Along with the other participants, ranging in age from three to eighty-three, those parents prayed, sang, and shared a meal together. They also listened to short talks and watched skits on the themes of the two events—the Virgin Mary and the Lamb of God. They learned about typology—how the Old Testament and the New Testament illuminate each other. They looked at sacred art, walked in a candlelight procession, and participated in question and answer sessions that enabled older members of the parish to teach younger members. They did those things because of the children, and many learned what they would never otherwise have learned.

Other parishes have found different ways to achieve similar results. At St. Thomas Aquinas in Camas, Washington, Father Lappe hosted talks for the parents in the Church while the children and teens' religious education programs went on in the school.

In Sacramento, when children make their First Confession, the parents are not only expected to attend the sacrament, but receive it as well. Instruction is offered beforehand, reminding parents what a "good Confession" entails, then each member of the family in turn makes their Confession.

And in Bossier City, Louisiana, Micah Murphy has a team of parents whose mission is not to work with the teens, but to reach out to other parents of teens, helping them understand the importance of involving their children in the youth group and teaching them how they can follow up with their teens at home.

Key to all these efforts is relationship building—finding ways to meet and befriend the parents of children in religious education programs or youth groups, parents who know enough about their faith to bring their children to receive the sacraments, but have forgotten (or never knew) why that was important. When those relationships are forged, religious education programs can offer priests and catechists more than just opportunities to form children. They offer them the opportunity to form entire families.

Preach the Whole Gospel

The last, but certainly not the least, of the essentials is this: Never preach anything less than the truth, the whole truth, and nothing but the truth . . . so help you God. That essential underlies every other essential described in this chapter.

Regardless of what we do at the parish level or in the culture, we must remember that evangelizing the culture never means compromising with the culture. Why? Just ask Jim Gontis, Director of Religious Education for the Diocese of Harrisburg.

"We're hardwired for the truth," says Gontis. "And watering down the faith works against us. An easy message may attract people at first but, in the end, it doesn't get them anywhere."

Over several years under the leadership of Bishop Kevin Rhoades, now Bishop of Fort Wayne-South Bend, the diocese experienced a renewal on just about every front—liturgical, catechetical, and devotional. On Divine Mercy Sunday, the cathedral is now packed for Mass, and long lines for Confession last throughout the day. Every summer, one hundred young men between the ages of fifteen and twenty-five, spend a week in seminary discerning their vocation and going deeper in the faith. Not surprisingly, the number of seminarians is on the rise.

The key to it all has been solid teaching, by solid teachers, using solid resources. They haven't used a lot of fancy techniques. They've simply taught people about the fatherhood of God and the role of the Blessed Mother. They've stressed the importance of the one, holy, and apostolic Church in God's plan for salvation. They've instructed people about mortal and venial sin, about our need for sanctifying grace, about the necessity of going to Confession, and about the graces that come from receiving the Eucharist.

They've given people what the culture is not giving them—truth. And they have not given them what the culture does give them—lies. Parishes and schools where the truth is preached see attendance at daily Mass go up, lines for Confession grow longer, and the collection basket grow heavier. More marriages last, more babies are born, and more young people are protected from the ravages of the culture. All of that happens because truth is what we're made for, and truth is what we want. We recognize it when we see it, and we respond to it. There are souls so damaged by sin that truth bounces off their hearts and minds, leaving barely a mark, but those souls are fewer and more far between than we might sometimes think. Most people want truth. Our job is to give it to them and let Christ do the rest.

***

Love the people you evangelize. Be a witness. Make the parish the curriculum. Embrace the new media. Build Catholic identity. Respect time. Engage the whole family. And preach the whole Gospel.

Those are the eight essentials of the new evangelization. Each principle is rooted in the specific needs and struggles of twenty-first century Americans and twenty-first century American Catholics. Each principle is tailored to meet those needs and address those struggles. Each principle is tailored to help the Gospel be heard today, here and now.

How each principle is applied will differ from parish to parish. These are principles, not programs. And they are not the only principles that can help dioceses, parishes, and schools carry out the new evangelization in their corner of the kingdom. But they are the most important. Again, they are the essentials. If we neglect one, in one way or another, our efforts will fall short.

CHAPTER 6

From Planning to Doing:
Taking the New Evangelization to the Streets

You've probably noticed that I haven't given you a list of programs to help you and your parish carry out the new evangelization. And I'm not going to. That's because in the new evangelization there's only one program that matters: Christ.

It really is that simple or, at least, it's that simple when we keep it that simple. American Catholics, like Americans in general, love a good program and all that goes with it—committees, budgets, planning. But far too often over the past several decades, we've loved those programs at the expense of *the* program—Jesus. We've let committees and budgets and plans get in the way of doing what we're supposed to do. We've allowed the needs of the program to direct us, rather than the needs of the people we're supposed to be evangelizing.

For the new evangelization to work—not just in a few parishes or schools, but everywhere in this country—priests and catechists have to figure out how to do what we're doing more creatively, more faithfully, and more effectively. Are we speaking and teaching and *scheduling* in such a way that we actually reach people? Are we faithfully carrying out the primary tasks assigned to us by the Church—administering the sacraments, teaching the faithful, and serving the community? Are we showing people what the faith has to say about the way they live their lives daily, about the things they care about the most?

That doesn't mean we don't implement new Bible studies or lecture series. Of course we do. New programs will often be necessary. But the program shouldn't be the focus of our efforts. The focus should be on *how* we do what we do. When we assess current parish and school programs, and when we look to develop new ones, our orientation should be toward evangelization, toward bringing people closer to Christ. That means determining whether or not current programs do that and, if not, figuring out how we can remedy the situation.

That's what the people in the stories from the last chapter did. That's what they're doing still. And that's why their efforts bear fruit. They don't think like bureaucrats. They think like evangelists. We all need to think like evangelists. That's our call.

But where does that call lead? Where should this rethinking of our vocation and parish life take us? Not just to a reawakening of faith among the baptized. And not just to the revitalization of the Catholic Church in our communities, dioceses, and country. Ultimately, as we've said before, it should lead to a renewed and transformed culture, to an America where human dignity is respected, human life treasured, and human solidarity is understood. It should lead to a society governed by Christian humanism, to a culture of life.

But for that to happen, we need to take one more step. The evangelized must become the evangelizers.

Reforming Formation

In 1990, the United States Bishops released a document on evangelization called *Heritage and Hope*, in which they proposed two phases of evangelization for the Church in America. The first phase is for all Catholics to become aware of our need "for being evangelized afresh, for bringing the light of Christ to our own lives and to those of our families and faith communities." The second phase, they continued, involved, "reaching out to alienated Catholics, the un-churched, and society at large with the Good News."[1]

Those phases both are and are not linear. On the one hand, until we Catholics have our own house in order—that is, until we know, believe, and live our faith—trying to preach the Good News to those outside the Church is an almost impossible task. After all, who will believe us if we don't first believe ourselves? On the other hand, the Christian life is always one of ongoing conversion. In this life, we never

---

[1] National Catholic Conference of Bishops/United States Catholic Conference, "Observance of the Quincentenary in the United States," in *Pastoral Letters and Statements of the United States Catholic Bishops 1989–97*, Vol. VI (Washington, D.C.: United States Catholic Conference, Inc., 1998), 257–58.

fully arrive at our destination. We're always learning, always growing, always falling, repenting, and getting up again. If we wait until every one of us is a canonized saint before we reach out to the larger culture, we'll be waiting an awfully long time. So, we don't wait. We do both at the same time. Or, rather, we do the latter—evangelize the culture—by doing the former—evangelizing Catholics.

And we do need to reach out to the larger culture. The train of secular humanism has left the station and is hurling the culture to a dangerous and deadly end. Like it or not, it's up to us, by God's grace, to stop it. And when I say "us," I'm not just talking about priests or catechists or anyone else who is part of the hierarchical or institutional structure of the Church. I'm talking about *all* Catholics—about teenagers and grandparents and dockworkers and accountants. The Church, as an institution, can only reach so far. She can only get her voice heard in so many places. But the Church, as the Body of Christ, made up of all the baptized, can go everywhere, with no limits on her reach. This, again, is why the second phase of evangelization called for by the bishops—the evangelization of the culture at large—depends more on the formation of the lay faithful than it does on anything else.

Doing the Essentials

So, where does this transformation of the evangelized into evangelizers begin?

It begins by applying the eight principles listed in the last chapter to our own and our parish's or school's work. We love the people we're evangelizing. We witness to the truth of what we teach with our actions and lives. We use every aspect of parish life—the Mass, homilies, devotions, service projects, even architecture—to hand on the faith. We help people come to see themselves first and foremost as Catholics. We use the Internet and the rest of the mass media to get our message out. We find creative times and places to preach the Gospel. We look for ways to evangelize whole families at a time. And in all of that, we never compromise the truth of what we preach.

Helping the evangelized become evangelizers really does begin with helping them not only to know and live their faith, but to be passionate about it. When Christ is the center of our life, when our relationship with Him is our greatest treasure, we can't help but want to share that with others. There can be no effective evangelization without passion. And passion—passion for Christ, for His Church, for His truth—is what those eight principles aim to produce.

But where does that beginning begin? We can't just wave a magic wand and have all eight principles perfectly integrated into the life of our parishes. That integration itself has to begin somewhere. So where? Assessment and planning.

Yes, I did begin this very chapter with a call for Catholics to think more like evangelists and less like bureaucrats. And yes, assessment and planning are two words that smack of politburo bureaucracies. But they don't have to play out that way in real life.

In *Thy Kingdom Come*, the U.S. Bishops called for each parish to establish an "evangelization team" to assess and direct the parish's evangelization efforts. They then entrusted these teams with three tasks:

1. Reviewing the catechetical efforts of the parish in light of the goal of evangelization and assessing the level of commitment of active Catholics in the parish;
2. Creating strategies to ensure that the parish remain focused on its mission to evangelize;
3. Training Catholics for outreach work.[2]

The success of these teams depends on whether or not they can avoid the normal pitfalls of committees. If they can, this kind of evangelization team can be an effective tool in reorienting a parish to the work of evangelization. In other words, as long as the pastor doesn't abdicate his authority to the committee, as long as the committee doesn't become focused on inner issues of power or control, and as long as their meetings are oriented toward action—and not more meetings—these evangelization teams can work.

---

[2] United States Catholic Conference of Bishops, Committee on Evangelization, "Conversion of Society," in *Thy Kingdom Come, a Manual for Diocesan Evangelization* (Washington D.C.: USCC, 1996), 9–11.

When it comes to task number one on that list—assessment—the teams need to ask certain questions, including:

- Do we combat the moral and religious pluralism that the culture preaches?

- Do we communicate the universal call to evangelize?

- Do our faith formation efforts include some basic introduction to philosophy, the type of philosophy required to see the errors of relativism and religious pluralism?

- Do they also include some elemental training in apologetics, enabling people to understand how the Church defends herself against common attacks?

- Do the faithful understand the Church's social teaching, so that they can advocate for Gospel values in the public square?

- Do we give them the tools necessary to grow in holiness as well as knowledge? What kind of spiritual formation does the parish provide?

- And most important of all, do our efforts bring people into a living relationship with Jesus Christ?

If the answer to any of those questions is "no," the next task on the list is to figure out why. Are the catechists poorly trained or do they possess a flawed understanding of the faith? Are the catechetical materials full of theological errors? Is the timing of parish events and programs a problem—are we working against and not with people's busy schedules? Are opportunities for formation and service too limited? Do we provide enough resources to help people learn about the faith on their own time? Do we miss opportunities to evangelize? Is there any way in which we don't think with the Church? Do we not address the problems people face in living out their faith in contemporary culture? Are we disconnected from the culture? Are we locked into doing things a certain way because "that's how they've always been done"?

Once those questions (and many more) have been answered, the process of planning and training can begin. That process might involve getting rid of some programs and adding new ones. It also could involve staffing changes or implementing catechist formation workshops. It often will involve looking for better materials and resources, finding new ways to communicate with parishioners, perhaps setting about that all-important website redesign, overhauling the music used in the liturgy, physical improvements to the church and the sanctuary, and even, for priests, some soul searching about whether we're really celebrating the Mass according to the mind of the Church.

The planning and training process also will involve ensuring that the formation programs in our parishes are not *ad hoc*, not just seasonal things. If evangelizing is *the* mission of the Church, then formation programs that help carry out that mission need to be an ongoing part of parish life. That's not to say that the same Scripture study has to run for fifty-two straight weeks. But throughout the year, in some way, there needs to be continual and consistent opportunities for formation. Even the smallest, poorest, most sparsely staffed parishes can do this, if only through the priest delivering catechetical homilies every Sunday, celebrating the Mass with reverence, leading the people in regular devotions, and doing it all with love as a living witness to the truth he preaches.

Throughout the assessment and planning phase, different parishes with different situations will come up with different action plans that best suit their different needs. But through it all, regardless of what answers come forth or what plans arise, the focus must remain on Christ—proclaiming Christ, leading people to faith in Christ, and helping them mature in a relationship with Christ.

When Christ is the focus, grace will come, and our efforts, however imperfect they may be, will bear fruit in our parishes and the culture at large.

The Evangelized Evangelizers

We make this effort—assessing, planning, training— to save souls. We also make it to save the culture. The one helps accomplish the other.

The laity can go places no priest can go, and their voices are the ones that register the loudest in cultural debates about human dignity and social justice. The more equipped they are to spread the Good News, the more the culture will be transformed by it.

Of course, we first need to convince Catholics of that truth. In every parish, pews are lined with good people with good intentions who wouldn't dream of missing Mass on Sunday, but who also wouldn't dream of inviting a friend to join them. Some have bought into the culture's message that to share their faith with friends would be a violation of their friends' freedom of conscience. Others have concluded that religion, like politics, is simply not the subject of polite conversation.

The burden is on the parish to convince them that this is not the case, that in fact they have a moral imperative to share their faith, draw others to the faith, and take their faith into the public square. Doing that is not merely the work of a Sunday homily. Nor is it simply the work of weekend workshop or a six-week parish program on evangelization. That understanding—of the necessity of evangelization and of all believers being evangelizers—has to permeate a parish or school's entire faith formation curriculum. If we are not forming people to both see the universal truth of the Gospel *and* embrace their baptismal vocation, we are not doing our job.

One of the most important ways we can convey that understanding is to correct a common misconception about where a deepened or renewed faith should lead.

In the years since Vatican II, many of the laity who have experienced an awakening of their faith have expressed that newfound enthusiasm by taking on liturgical or ministerial roles in the Church. They sign up to become readers or extraordinary ministers of Holy Communion; they seek employment as catechists or youth ministers; and they volunteer their time doing corporal works of mercy in the parish. The visibility of lay faithful in ministry has strengthened how the Church pursues her mission. The Church very much needs well-trained lay people working side by side with clergy to pass on the faith and assist in all the daily tasks of running a parish, school, or diocese. And, of course, the life of faith demands corporal works of mercy.

But parish and diocesan faith formation programs must stress that the primary way Catholics are called to live their vocation is by faithfully carrying out the duties of their state in life and witnessing to the Gospel in the home, the workplace, and the culture. Lay people simply do more good for the Church by living their faith in the office among co-workers than by reading at Mass on Sundays.

It's equally important for a parish to stress to its parishioners that the primary evangelizers of the culture will always be them, not the institutional arms of the Church, because effective evangelization occurs person to person. It occurs when someone who does not know Jesus sees a believer practicing his faith, deriving strength from it, and loving others because of it. It occurs when a Catholic is available to help out a co-worker or a family member struggling with questions of meaning. It occurs when we invite a person to come to Mass with us, come to a Bible study with us, or check out the RCIA process at our parish.

It also occurs when Catholics work to create a social and political order in which faith can take root and grow.

When the laws of a nation do not respect life and the dignity of the human person, a chain reaction occurs. A culture of violence and radical individualism takes root. Families break up, people break down, and huge psychological barriers to the faith take hold. People struggle to hear truth because of the change it demands of them and because their own sins and struggles stop their ears and shut their eyes.

That's what we see all around us. The more Catholics take an active role in countering the structures of sin generated and propped up by unjust laws, the easier our work of evangelizing the culture will be. Likewise, the less of a role we take, the harder it will be.

Recently, Catholics have gotten a little better at this, but not much. The majority of Catholics who fill seats in the Senate and the House of Representatives, for as much as they may care about the poor and advocate for peace, are openly and adamantly pro-choice. On the most important, fundamental, and pressing political issue of our day, they stand in opposition to what the Church and the natural law teaches. Nearly 50 percent of Catholics who vote have no problem with the stand these politicians take on abortion—at least not enough of a problem to cast their vote differently. Other Catholics remain as unfamiliar with what the Church teaches about the principles of subsidiarity, solidarity, and the preferential option for the poor as they do with formulas for nuclear fission. Still more keep silent, despite knowing the truth, because of wrong-headed notions about the separation of religion and politics, believing that faith has no place in public policy debates.

The bishops of our country have said over and over again (and rightly so) that the Catholic Church does not align itself with any one political party or candidate. The Church isn't seeking to create a monolithic voting bloc. But some issues matter more than others, and one issue matters more than anything else. When Catholics act otherwise, they cause confusion and scandal. That's why clearly communicating the Church's social teaching and the imperative for Catholics to act according to it—living on Monday what they profess on Sunday—is as integral to a parish's evangelization efforts as any apologetics workshop or philosophy lecture.

While bishops and priests have the role of being the primary teachers of our faith, handing on what the Gospel instructs us, the role of the lay faithful resides more in the temporal and social orders of society. This means that the laity has as their vocation the responsibility of consistently living their Catholic faith in the midst of the world. As a senator, mechanic, parent, doctor, electrician, CEO—each are called to simply be faithful and allow their faith to form judgments, decisions, and actions. Culture becomes all that God intends when truth is lived according to the traditions of that culture. Faith is not in opposition to culture; rather, it allows culture to be everything it can be.

The Evangelizing Church

Evangelization is most effective when it is personal. Jesus Christ personally touched the lives of people. Lives were changed when people heard the Good News preached by the apostles. The Holy Spirit blesses the Body of Christ with charisms, offices, and institutions needed to grow the Church and preserve the Gospel in whatever situations we find ourselves. But in the end, the personal conviction of clergy, religious, and lay faithful is what arouses in others the curiosity to be open to movement of the Holy Spirit.

I had the unique privilege of serving as personal secretary to Pittsburgh's former bishop, now Cardinal Donald Wuerl, the Archbishop of Washington, D.C., shortly after my ordination. I learned firsthand the effectiveness of how a pastor of souls can bring about so much change by being courageous, direct, and hands-on in carrying out the mission of the Church. I won't get into too much detail in order to preserve confidentiality, but the conversions that took place among business and community leaders, laws that were changed because of the bishop's unwavering convictions, and how the diocese would conduct its business in the wider community, all have influenced my own passion for evangelization. The Catholic Church in Pittsburgh is well respected by the civic, political, business, and ecumenical communities because the bishop allowed himself to be the pastor of everyone. Faithfully preaching the Gospel, bringing the Church into the social and temporal realities of life, and allowing ministry to be really effective, is how then Bishop Wuerl carried out his ministry in Pittsburgh. Surely this is the work of the Holy Spirit, but I do not find it coincidental that nearly thirty thousand people were initiated into the Catholic Church in his eighteen years as our bishop. I am sure that through his own quiet yet persistent manner, great things are happening for the Church of Washington, D.C.

In *The Church Alive,* his first pastoral letter, Bishop David Zubik, the current bishop and a native of Pittsburgh, has excited the base, as they say. Evangelization has become a priority for the diocese. The bishop clearly sees evangelization from its theological nature with pastoral implications. He is challenging priests to reclaim their identity and authority, calling upon the lay faithful to assume their proper place in society as their first task of living faith, asking that parishes evaluate how they celebrate the sacred liturgy according to the universal mind of the Church. It is no wonder that in his first year as bishop, vocations to the priesthood increased by a third. He has chosen to sell the bishop's mansion, opting to live with the seminarians as truly the spiritual father of these young men.

Starting from the top, with these two bishops and certainly our Holy Father, we see how the Church is an evangelizing community with pastors who exercise clear, strong leadership for service to the flock—pastors who know how to lovingly yet strongly exercise their pastoral authority. It requires deacons who make a difference in the lives of people; consecrated sisters and brothers not afraid to live out their community's charisms; seminarians who choose to live the gift of celibacy as a sign of freedom and love; married couples not practicing artificial birth control and creating a household of prayer and virtue; college students who choose to pray before the Blessed Sacrament on a Friday night rather than party; and more and more single folks who see their lives as a vocation for building up the Kingdom in their service to culture. The evangelizing Church needs teams of seniors who pray day after day for the welfare of the Church using those rosary beads with fingers marked with holiness. The new evangelization begins with *our* own efforts within the Church. Great things are happening when we listen and respond to the Holy Spirit.

How we relate to the wider community is also just as important for the evangelization of culture. Topping the list of work the Church can do to evangelize the culture is the Church's social ministry in the community. Pope Benedict's recent encyclical *Caritas in Veritate* once again reminds us that the Body of Christ lives within the world and must consider all the social problems of man when proclaiming the Gospel in all its totality. From ecology to economy, the Church must allow the Gospel to be effective, understood, and applicable to the new situations in which our world finds itself. Otherwise, the Church and the Gospel are seen as unimportant and certainly with no meaning when disconnected from man's woes. Indeed, while the Gospel is not a roadmap for social solutions, it keeps us grounded in truth so that the solutions man considers are not in contradiction to the truth.

The Church serves because we are called to love. Caring for people is not primarily a means to an end. Feeding the homeless, caring for the elderly, educating children, and performing any number of other corporal works of mercy, demonstrates the presence of God in the world and the power of faith that no sin or darkness can thwart.

As the culture changes, of course, so will its needs. Parishes and dioceses must continually evaluate whether the ministry programs they have in place correspond to the needs of the community. Are the needs primarily corporal? In other words, do people need food, clothing, housing, help with childcare, or assistance paying their heating bills? Or are the needs spiritual? Is the affluence of the community leading to teenage drug use and experimental types of promiscuity? Do families need help prioritizing their time and spending? Are marriages unstable? Changing demographics also should be considered. Is the local population aging? Becoming more ethnically diverse? Are more young families moving in?

Asking these questions enables us to identify the needs that are to be met, not the needs we think ought to be met. In turn, that helps us bear more effective witness to Christ in our communities.

In *Encounters with Faith*, the bishops also counsel parishes to evaluate their own attitude towards outsiders. Do they invite people to "come and see" the faith—hosting open houses and advertising inquiry nights? Do they welcome new members to the parish, introduce them to other parishioners, and look for ways to connect them into the life of the parish? Do they reach out through schools, local media, and other venues to call people into the Church? Do they create opportunities for those who are seeking to find answers?[3]

Finally, the institutional Church can help evangelize the culture by publicly addressing the life of the larger culture—from politics and economics to teen music and fashion trends. Since the Church exists to evangelize, and all men exist to be evangelized, every element of human activity concerns her. Homilies and bulletin inserts, statements from the local bishop, and documents issued by the United States Catholic Conference of Bishops are all ways the Church can address these issues, modeling for individual Catholics the role they must play

---

[3] United States Catholic Conference of Bishops, "Invitation to Inactive Catholics and Unchurched Peoples," in *Encounters with Faith* (Washington D.C.: USCC, 1991), 18.

in the public square—speaking truth and making the position of the Church clearly known.

***

Two thousand years ago, the Roman Empire was not converted by memorandums. It was converted by deacons, priests, and bishops who proclaimed and lived the truth without fail. And it was converted by men and women who imaged Christ in the world. So many of those early Christians were martyred for their love of Christ. They also loved the Church. There can be no complete and authentic evangelization without our love for the Church, which embodies Jesus Christ in word and sacrament. What we saw at the outset of the Church, especially in the pages of the New Testament, were men and women who witnessed to what they saw and believed.

These early Christians often celebrated liturgy in secret to keep the faith alive, practiced chastity and fidelity in their marriages, and cared for the poor with their limited resources. And like their deacons, priests, and bishops, they died for the truth. Doctrine mattered to them as much as virtuous living. They found the right balance between knowledge and love, between proclaiming with words and proclaiming with deeds.

In some ways, it's not quite that easy anymore. Dioceses need catechetical curriculum review committees and information technology departments. Task forces, *ad hoc* committees, and deanery meetings are corporate ways for the Church to advance the mission of the Gospel. There are also parish and diocesan politics to navigate and egos to massage, not to mention wrong-headed ways of understanding and living the faith that are deeply entrenched in many parishes. Those problems can't be reversed by a royal edict from any deacon, priest, bishop, or pastoral council. They require patience, diplomacy, and a keen sense of which battles we pick and when. That's our reality. We have to work within it.

But in other ways evangelization is so easy. People still need Christ. Christians continue to see the relationship between faith and culture. The energy seen in youth who spent summers on a mission trip; seminarians energized in wanting to preach the Gospel; newlywed couples who take their faith seriously; the Holy Father welcoming young people from all over the world to meet with him—all of these experiences are expressions of the new evangelization, how faith is being lived in culture, and how culture truly becomes what God intended.

That's why thinking of evangelization as an orientation, not an item on a checklist, as a theological mystery, not a program for implementation, is so important. It helps us weigh all the structures we use to reach our goal in terms of the goal, not in terms of the structures themselves.

When we think that way, when we act that way, the new evangelization becomes a shared mission among all Catholics. It is something tangible that a parish pastoral council can embrace, a direction a bishop can lead his staff, a goal for individual families at home.

CONCLUSION

The Missing Variable and the Sum Total

The Church exists in order to evangelize. Man exists in order to be evangelized.

Every priest, every catechist, every teacher, and every Catholic needs to sear those two truths into their memory. When we forget either, we cannot be who we're called to be, and we cannot do what we're called to do. Evangelization is not simply a part of the Church's mission, a program to which we can devote one office in a diocese or one committee in our parish and call it good. It is the very reason why the Church exists. And through it, she helps man come to find the reason for his existence. She gives him the answer to the perennial questions, "Who am I?" and "Why am I here?"

The title of this book is *The Church's Mission in America: Making Sense of the New Evangelization*. At the outset, I took a very mathematical approach, arguing that "who" is being evangelized and "what" evangelization is, add up to "how" the Church can carry out the new evangelization. And to a certain extent that's true. The Church can't evangelize the men and women living in this day and age without understanding them—their hopes, their fears, their struggles, and their strengths. And evangelization only works when we understand it not as a program, but as the theological basis of why we have a Church and why God has revealed Himself to us—a theological concept whose boundaries are set by the soteriological, christological, ecclesiological, and anthropological foundations of the faith.

Pope John Paul II used the expression "the new evangelization" to implement the vision of the Second Vatican Council. He assured us of the unchanging theological realities confirmed in the Spirit by the Church while also positioning the Church to respond adequately, forcefully, and effectively to the circumstances of the present age. The "new evangelization" does not cause divisions within the Church when the Gospel is embraced in its totality and then faithfully preached. The era following the Second Vatican Council saw a misrepresentation of the intentions of the Council Fathers, who neither wanted the Church to remain disconnected from the problems of modern man nor disregard Tradition for purposes of being pastoral and relevant.

Without a theological framework to define and understand evangelization, people will design their own definitions. Wrong definitions can cause great harm in a parish and diocese. The tail wagging the dog is when the Church allows social conditions to dictate the mission of the Church. The mission has been well defined by Jesus Christ—*teach and baptize all nations.* The Magisterium of the Church will ensure that clergy, religious, and lay faithful carry out that mission well grounded in what God has revealed to us.

My reflection has identified the four theological foundations for evangelization: the soteriological, christological, ecclesiological, and anthropological. The relationship between faith and culture creates the dynamism between how the grace of God and the initiative of man makes the Kingdom of God a reality, something tangible. We often refer to this lived experience as Christian humanism, as discussed earlier, in which all mankind benefits from how the Catholic Church succeeds in manifesting the Kingdom of God by living in accord with the Sacred Scriptures, Tradition, doctrine, and the liturgy.

When Christians understand that ultimately our efforts in living the Gospel and preaching the Good News result in conversion only because of the Holy Spirit, we come to humbly acknowledge that God invites us to be partners in manifesting His Kingdom. When we forget about God's initiative in divine Revelation, we are left with polemics, ideologies, and ultimately failure. Evangelization is a human encounter with mystery, not a formula of activity. The unfolding of that mystery— in our lives, our parishes, and our culture—demands something that none of us can produce on our own: *grace.*

Every time the Word is heard and embraced, grace, not man, accomplishes that miracle. And every time a heart gives itself in love and obedience to Jesus, grace, not man, deserves the applause. It is

God's grace, and no formula devised by ecclesiocrats, that has enabled the Church for two thousand years to go about making disciples of all nations. And it is God's grace and God's grace alone that will enable the new evangelization to be anything more than a clever title given to just another man-made, man-run effort.

We still have our part to play. We have to cooperate with that grace and be open to it. We cannot reduce the work of evangelization to a human construct. Nor can we reduce divine Revelation to anything less than the fullness of what the Church has passed down through the centuries. If we constrict the mystery of God in an attempt to make it more palatable to our modern, post-modern culture, we block the pathways of grace. Few of us have to look far to see the truth of that. How many of our parish programs have failed because a theologian, a homilist, a catechist, or even a parent has tried to squeeze the Gospel into a human story and explain away the mystery, costing the Gospel its force, its boldness, and its freshness?

No, any attempts on our part to compromise the mystery will cost us the mystery. That is a cost countless parishes and universities are paying today. They pay it in the diminished or lost faith of the souls in their charge—a payment that in the end costs all of us.

We cooperate with grace when we preach and practice the fullness of truth, when we witness to it with our words and actions. But one thing more is necessary, one thing that makes that preaching and practicing possible: *prayer*. We cannot receive God's grace nor can our work be a channel for God's grace, if we're not asking for grace. The words we speak, the programs we plan, and the liturgies we celebrate must be rooted in prayer. When they're not, it shows. Maybe not at first, but eventually the fruit tells all there is to know about the tree.

***

John Paul II began his pontificate with a charge to the faithful: "Be not afraid." At the Mass marking the start of his pontificate, Benedict XVI issued the same charge: "Be not afraid of Christ. He takes away nothing and gives all."

As a Church, as a body of believers, we must heed that charge. We must not be afraid to proclaim Christ, in all His mystery and majesty, to the world. We must not be afraid to proclaim Christ to our own, either. We must do our part regarding the things we can control, and trust that God will take care of the rest.

There is so much fear in our world today. There is so much fear in each of us: fear of failing, of being rejected, of making waves and ruffling feathers. There is fear of being unpopular, of being thought extreme. There is fear of losing parishioners and losing students, fear of the collection baskets coming back empty and capital campaign goals going unmet.

Those aren't foolish fears. Of course we all want to be successful, we don't want to drive people away, and we certainly want to keep the lights on. What is foolish is to think that compromising the truth in what we say and do will prevent those fears from becoming realities. For a few years or even decades it might seem like things are working, but in the end, compromise will cost us everything. It's already costing us plenty, as pews empty and parishes close despite pastors' best efforts to accommodate the Gospel to the culture's demands.

If the new evangelization asks anything of us, it is to "be not afraid." We must not be afraid of what will come of us when we step forward in faith. We must not be afraid of putting into practice all the wisdom the Church has given us about evangelization. We must not be afraid to give people the deepest desires of their heart, to give people a reason to live and to live fully, and to give them the very means by which they live. By which we all live.

As long as we pray, as long as we love, as long as we strive to do God's will, grace will come and fruit will burst forth. If we move forward innocent as doves and wise as serpents, the faithful will grow stronger and bolder. The Church will be renewed and the culture healed.

There is no greater love than this: to lay down your life for a friend (Jn. 15:13). Speaking these words to His apostles, Christ, who indeed did lay down His life, gave us a model of ministry in Himself. In doing so, in obedience to the Father's plan, salvation has come to the world. We, who are baptized in the saving mysteries of Christ, share and extend salvation to others when our faith is lived in the same generous and loving way that God has done in Jesus Christ. The culture of death will pass away to the civilization of love.

We see this in the person of Christ. Death gave way to life. The Church brings life to our cultures through word and sacrament, and by the witness of those who bear the name of Christ: the Christian. Yes, disciples left Jesus. Yes, apostles betrayed Him and were reluctant to profess their faith. Yet, the faith professed by Peter is the faith on which the Church has been established. In fact, the Church not only is built upon Peter's faith, but upon Peter himself. We are the Body of Christ, and the gates of hell shall not prevail against us!